Billion-Dollar Branding

Billion-Dollar Branding

Brand Your Small Business Like A Big-Business
And Make Great Things Happen

HONEY PARKER & BLAINE PARKER

Foreword by Dave Lakhani

New York

Billion-Dollar Branding

Brand Your Small Business Like A Big-Business And Make Great Things Happen

ISBN 978-1-61448-272-7 paperback
ISBN 978-1-61448-273-4 eBook
Library of Congress Control Number: 2012935463

Morgan James Publishing
The Entrepreneurial Publisher
5 Penn Plaza, 23rd Floor,
New York City, New York 10001
(212) 655-5470 office • (516) 908-4496 fax
www.MorganJamesPublishing.com

Interior Design by:
Bonnie Bushman
bonnie@caboodlegraphics.com

This book is for all the small businesses owners with whom we've worked who have been brave enough to commit. They're much happier and more profitable for it. (As a result, so are we.)

REALLY IMPORTANT NOTE

This book is about a very controversial subject: branding a business. There is a tremendous amount of disagreement about what branding is. There is also a tremendous amount of disagreement about what branding does. That aside, there is plenty of protected brand imagery. This book deals with the creation of brand. It does not deal with the legal ramifications of branding, infringing on registered trademarks, and other areas of brand liability. As with any such endeavor, you require the services of a good attorney in order to stay out of trouble. Do not expect this book to help you in that regard. Do not call us when George Lucas sues you for infringing on the rights of his Star Wars franchise when you open alien-themed Wookie Cookies in your local strip mall. We are not lawyers. We are marketers. Get representation. May the force of good legal know-how be with you.

TABLE OF CONTENTS

FOREWORD

Just about every day, I'm asked to write the foreword to a book. Most days, I simply say no, even to friends. The answer to why is that I don't want to be branded as a professional foreword writer. When Blaine and Honey approached me and asked me to consider writing this foreword, I said, "Maybe. Let me read the book."

They sent it and I started reading. I consumed the book in a day and set it aside, but kept coming back to it. There was something that I couldn't immediately put my finger on, but it kept pulling me back. I had to know more. I could sense there was magic in the words that I hadn't read before; and I had to understand what the magic was, and if it could be profitably and universally applied to small businesses.

Then it hit me. This book is the antidote to everything that is wrong with the plethora of marketing books on business owners' bookshelves today. It doesn't offer plug-in, fill-in-the-blank worksheets that promise you a fantastical brand and tagline that is sure to appeal to the ethos, pathos and logos each of us are silently craving. It doesn't give you a detailed analysis of the world's biggest brands simply to demonstrate what can be done if you have a big enough budget.

The book tackles, head-on, the idea that branding is a waste and direct response marketing is the only answer to attracting a buying consumer today . . . Blaine and Honey also demonstrate how brand can make direct response more responsive.

They pull out the holy grail of small business advertising and they crap all over it.

There, I said it.

The thing that kept pulling me back was their very direct confrontation of the status quo. But not just confrontation for the sake of being provocative. Blaine and Honey lay bare the consumer influence genome. Most importantly of all, they give you the tools through both rhetoric and example to discover it in yourself (and your clients) to affect you profitably and forever.

Inside this book, you'll experience an onion being peeled back layer by layer. You'll learn through examples of large businesses you know, but more often small businesses like yours that you don't. You'll learn exactly how brands are discovered and translated into an experience that the consumer can embody and extol.

What you won't find in this book is a list of colors and how they make you feel.

There is no long discussion of the relative merit of dozens of font styles.

You will find a discussion about why making your logo bigger in an ad is mostly stupid.

For the last few years, pundits have been talking about the eminent demise of traditional media and the dominance of social media. I've been writing and preaching that social media is the media, too. It isn't any different—it's simply a different distribution channel. Inside these pages you won't find a long love affair with social media. But they do demonstrate exactly how your brand can be most effectively distributed through the medium. This is a great departure from the hundreds of books being published today about social media and the "godsend" it promises to be. Don't get me (or Blaine and Honey) wrong: social media is a force to be understood and mastered. But it follows a set of brand rules that Blaine and Honey lay out which remain unchanged, regardless of the medium.

In this book, you're invited to ask hard questions about yourself, your business and your customer – and they expect you to answer them thoughtfully. But thinking alone won't do the trick. They urge you to analyze, consider, test and create. They challenge your fear and ego, and you won't like it one bit. It's going to scare you, you won't want to do it, you'll protest that your business is different (it isn't). But, in the end, if you listen to the book's message, your business will be transformed, and so will your customer.

This is a book about creating a customer experience that puts the customer first; a book that understands that customers want to be moved and connected to something they can believe in. They want that old-time religion—an experience that they have to tell someone else about because it touched them at their very core.

What do Andrew Dice Clay, Lisa Lampanelli and Jeff Foxworthy have to do with branding? It turns out, quite a bit. If I told you one was a drummer, one a Harvard grad and one a graduate from one of the top ten undergrad programs in the United States, would you be able to tell me who's who? Of course not. But if I say "Hickory Dickory Dock", or "You might be a redneck if…", or "Usually I'm on top to keep the guy from escaping," you'll likely be able to attribute it immediately to the correct comic. Not because of their educational or experiential background, but because they understand what their brand is and to whom it appeals—and they deliver with ruthless efficiency.

What I love best about this book are the Ignition Points at the end of each chapter, giving you a very specific place to start your brand discovery process. Each ignition point builds, moving you from gathering fuel to building a roaring brand inferno that consumes competition and forges lifelong customers.

Be prepared. Blaine and Honey will practice a unique brand of tough love with you (as they do with their clients) throughout these pages. And you will inevitably ask the question, "How does this apply to me?" When you come upon that question, it's your cue to dig in, to suspend your fear and ego, to stow your preconceived notions and knowledge of marketing to date. Stick with it, examine, explore, question, and test. Your business will be transformed.

Read this book once to understand the concepts, and then go through it page by page, chapter by chapter, and do the work. Without doing the work, this book will be completely worthless to you. But if you do, success will not only be predictable, but certain.

Dave Lakhani
Author of *Persuasion: The Art of Getting What You Want & How To Sell When Nobody's Buying (and how to sell even more when they are)*
www.howtosellwhennobodysbuying.com
January, 2012
Boise, ID

PREFACE

Why "Billion-Dollar Branding?"

There's a lot of literature on branding.

There's also a lot of anti-branding sentiment.

The branding naysayers will tell you, "Branding is great if you're a multi-billion dollar company, but Joe's Pizza can't afford it."

We beg to differ.

If you're a small business, branding is your friend—perhaps even more so than if you're a billion-dollar company.

Billion-dollar companies can often make up for their branding mistakes simply by spending more money on media.

You and us, not so much.

However, the strategies and tactics that billion-dollar brands use to establish their identities and market themselves are entirely scalable to a small business—even a sole proprietorship.

It isn't about spending a billion dollars.

It's about doing the same kind of strategic thinking and hard work that goes into creating a billion-dollar brand.

You don't need to have a billion.

But with any luck, if you play your cards right, you can make a billion…

Chapter 1

THE PROBLEM WITH BRAND

What the hell IS brand, anyway?

Few know.

But everyone thinks they know.

What does everyone think they know?

Just ask around.

"Brand is a logo."

"I've branded my business with this color."

"In order to make sure my advertising is always branded, we use these five fonts and we say, "Bob's Miniature Widgets—for all your Miniature Widget needs."

"I've branded myself with this jingle. It's the music from 'Happy Birthday,' but the words are about linoleum."

"We branded this TV commercial harder by making the logo an inch and a half bigger than before."

Seriously. This is what many people think brand is all about.

And it's not like small business advertisers have a corner on this market.

Yes, the "Bob's Miniature Widget" example actually comes from things Blaine has heard small business advertisers say repeatedly.

But the notion of branding "harder" by making the logo bigger is the kind of thing Honey has heard marketing executives say when working on huge national advertising campaigns. Even when told that's not "branding harder," they say, "No, no, I know, but can you do it anyway?"

No matter the size of the business or the experience of the people involved, the definition of brand remains elusive.

It's like the blind men who are explaining what an elephant looks like—yet each of them is doing so by feeling only one part of the elephant. Everyone has some vague idea about a tiny piece of the branding puzzle, but they don't understand its integration into the whole. And brand is a whole. It's the sum of much smaller, well thought-out parts with a very specific goal.

As everyone knows, "If it's on Wikipedia, it must be true." Accordingly, Wikipedia comes a bit closer to getting the definition of brand right by saying that branding is "the identity of a specific product, service, or business."

And while that definition is a major step in the right direction, that's still not quite correct.

Clinically, it's accurate.

But customers aren't clinicians.

And your brand is aimed at your customers.

Which means that, like everything else about your marketing, a brand should be *about* your customers.

And if you know your Sales Philosophy 101, you know that customers do not make buying decisions intellectually. They make their buying decisions emotionally.

Once their emotions are triggered, they will use their intellect to justify the purchase. Human beings can justify almost anything if they want to. You just need to make them want to. (Within reason, of course. We're talking about keeping it all legal and ethical here.)

So, your customers need to be engaged emotionally.

Your customers need to feel something.

Therefore, if we follow the notion of brand to its logical conclusion, a brand is one thing and one thing only.

Your brand is the ***one*** way you want customers to ***feel*** about your business.

That's so significant, it bears repeating.

Your brand is the ***one*** way you want customers to ***feel*** about your business.

What do you think?

All the jingles, logos, taglines, colors, fonts, slow-motion kids with puppies playing in sprinklers, high-energy montages of tight-bodied athletes crossing the finish line, double-entendre headlines that are just a bit naughty—they all need to feed into the *one* way you want customers to *feel* about your business.

Is that tickling something back there in your marketing nether regions?

Does it make any sense to your gray matter?

Do we need to pull you out of the deep end of the pool and start again back at the splash pad?

Let's take a visit through the Land O' Brand.

Let's look at what makes a brand work, some stellar examples of brand, break down why they've been so successful, and figure out how to apply the concept of brand to your own business.

Then, at some point in our journey we'll discuss how you get to your logo, color, font, jingle, tagline, t-shirt, mug, bobble-head dolls, etcetera. Until then…

Get ready.

Tuck away any loose clothing and long hair, strap in and hang on. It's going to be a wild ride like Mr. Toad never imagined…

IGNITION POINTS

- Brand is not a color, a logo, a font or any other technical detail about a company's image.

- Branding "harder" is not about making a logo bigger, saying the name more often, or repeating some lame, meaningless phrase.
- Branding is defining your company's personality in a way that makes the customer feel something significant about the business.
- Emotions are key. People might justify a purchase intellectually—but they first decide to buy emotionally. So it is with your brand.

FIRESTARTER

It's possible you already consider your business to be branded. How do you define your business's brand? Does it hold water relative to the points mentioned above?

Chapter 2

WHAT IS BRAND *REALLY*?

Brand is the single most misunderstood concept in marketing.

It doesn't matter who you are or what you do, chances are pretty good that you have some opinion of what brand is—and it's probably wrong.

Even Blaine's mother, a retired successful business woman with an entrepreneurial streak, challenges our definition of brand because she believes her answer is right.

She believes a brand is the physical act of stamping a logo on something.

Sorry, Mom.

Now, if she meant that your brand is the act of stamping the *feeling* of your business into someone's psyche, she's not that far off. But you and I both know that's not what she meant.

She is also typical.

Folks, this is non-negotiable.

Brand is one thing and one thing only.

Brand is the ***one*** way you want customers to ***feel*** about your business.

And we can prove it.

How can we be so certain?

For one, we can document our assertions, which we are about to do.

For another, all kinds of people, from sole proprietors to actual, experienced marketing executives, have approached us after seeing our assertions and the supporting evidence, and said:

"I've never heard it put that succinctly."

"That's the most actionable assertion of brand I've ever come across."

"Here, have a cookie."

"Holy cow!"

Things like that.

Having the sole proprietors say this isn't too surprising. After all, they usually didn't go to school for this. They have professions like photography and massage therapy and diabetes counseling. They are specialists who know their specialty. They are not marketing professionals.

The marketing professionals, on the other hand, often find their heads spinning around. They say things like, "Wow! In the 20 years I've been doing this, nobody has ever made it so clear!"

And that's not surprising, either.

Because branding ultimately is a very simple, uncomplicated concept.

And like so many very simple, uncomplicated concepts, it takes an enormously long time to discover and master.

Possibly the only thing more difficult than defining the concept of branding is actually building a brand.

It's a bit like architecture.

It's easy to say, "Architecture is the science of designing and erecting buildings."

But actually doing it is not easy. It's incredibly complex.

It takes years of schooling and additional years of practice before one can be licensed as an architect.

And once you get there, it doesn't mean you're ever going to be a brilliant architect.

After all, look at all the truly hideous buildings out there. Or the ones that simply have no distinguishing characteristics.

What does a Frank Gehry or a Frank Lloyd Wright or an I.M. Pei have that a guy who should be designing strip malls, Trenton subdivisions and many of our great nation's slaughterhouses doesn't have?

Why do you look at a Frank Lloyd Wright home and go, "Holy Mother of Pearl!"

And then, why can you look at the house next to it and say, "So what?" Or worse, "Egad."

Here's a crazy guess: the good ones, the Wrights and the Peis and the Gehrys, are different because they know something.

They know a building is not about the materials or the square footage or the piece of land it's going on.

It's not about all the individual pieces, although quality matters.

They know a building is about the people who are going to use it.

People with heart, hope, and desire.

Suddenly, that changes everything about what architecture is.

Look at Frank Gehry's Disney Concert Hall, possibly one of the most celebrated works of contemporary architecture. Most theaters or concert halls, no matter how ornate and gussied up they may appear, are essentially a box that houses a stage.

The Disney Concert Hall is nothing like a box.

It's a series of soaring, complex curves that immediately captures your heart much in the way a great musical performance does.

Forgive this if it sounds somewhat simplistic, but people go there to be stirred. And their emotions are stirred before they ever enter the building.

You see the structure and you are instantly engaged by it. It's intensely difficult to see it and NOT feel something. The entire building is about the people who are going to use it: the musicians and the music lovers whose fascination defies convention.

After all, you can explain the technical aspects of music all day long—but technical details are no substitute for actually experiencing the music.

Moreover, you don't need to know anything about musical technique to be affected by it. All you need to do is hear it and feel it.

The Disney Concert Hall is the architectural equivalent of a soaring and complex song. Love it or hate it, it makes you feel something—and it is designed expressly for that purpose: to make you feel something distinct.

And it was done very calculatingly by an architect.

With that in mind, no longer is architecture merely "the science of designing and erecting buildings."

Suddenly, architecture is the art of connecting a building's design with both function and emotion.

Yes, it involves a lot of science and technical design principles.

It also involves doors and windows and walls and roofs. The pieces.

But even you can go out in your yard, erect some mud walls and a thatched roof and call it a building.

That doesn't make it architecture any more than a beaver dam is architecture.

Similarly, any business owner can go out and have an internet-based graphic designer slap together a logo for 50 bucks and call it a "brand."

That's brand about as much as your mud hut is architecture.

The few businesses that dominate the marketplace, that make their owners wealthy, that are top of mind for the consumers in their target demographic, they are the ones living in the Disney Concert Hall.

The vast majority of businesses are living in mud huts.

Why?

Because they don't understand brand as anything other than parts.

To truly have a brand requires understanding what the parts, including the ones you can't see, actually do to people.

Brand is not a logo, a font, a color or a jingle.

Brand is the ***one*** way you want people to ***feel*** about your business.

THAT'S ALL WELL AND GOOD—BUT I DON'T DO BRAND ADVERTISING

Ah, yes. That old bugaboo.

The one that's perpetrated by various practitioners of direct response advertising.

The one that says, "Brand advertising is a waste of time and money. What you need to do is direct response advertising with an offer and a call to action."

Uh-hunh.

Right.

So, if you have a strong brand, and that brand permeates all of your direct response efforts, that's not going to give you a leg up on a DR advertiser with no brand?

Here and now, we are going to do something that will seem unusual.

It will seem unusual because we, after all, are specialists in small business marketing.

And small business marketing specialists love to thrash big advertising agencies.

"They don't know what they're doing!"

That, my friends, is a load of crap.

Plenty of big advertising agencies know exactly what they're doing.

That's how some huge advertising agencies have helped create some high-tonnage gorillas of brand.

We'll be discussing a few of those brand gorillas later on.

For the moment, though, we need to dispel the notion that big agencies are clueless and brand advertising is irrelevant.

Many, many big agencies do brand quite well.

If you happen to see lousy brand advertising out there, there's a chance one of two things has happened.

One, the big agency really is clueless.

Or two, and more likely, the advertiser is unmanageable.

Ah, yes. The advertiser.

The party known as the agency's "client."

Blaine has spent about two decades working with small businesses and creating their advertising.

Honey has spent about two decades working with big agencies, creating advertising for big businesses.

Here now, the common denominator between those two worlds, which also happens to be a primary stumbling block to creating good advertising: the client.

There are plenty of clients who let good advertising happen.

Unfortunately, there are also clients who refuse to let good advertising happen.

They will stand in the way of everything that comes down the pike.

They become a de facto Advertising Prevention Department.

At some point, the agency has no choice but to do exactly what that client wants, regardless of how wrong it might be.

That is where so much lousy advertising grows from.

The problem is not big agencies.

The problem is the same as it has always been since the beginning of time.

The problem is people.

People come pre-packaged with fear & ego. Fear & ego are the two biggest killers of quality, clarity and effectiveness.

In fact, most writers and art directors in big ad agencies have a file somewhere in their office filled with great ads that were never produced. Solid, quality work that never got to see the light of day—usually because the client was (a) afraid or (b) had "a better idea." There are even award competitions for these ads. (In fact, Blaine has a radio commercial for women's underwear that won a Silver Microphone Award for "Best Spot That Never Made It To Air." It scared a lot of people around the radio station. The client said, "It's not edgy enough." Fear, meet ego.)

When a Hollywood star burns through ten personal assistants in five years, it's safe to assume the celebrity is an unmanageable ass who makes life a living hell for these people. We are much less likely to blame the employee than we are to blame the employer.

But there's a noted brand of imported beer that's had six different ad agencies in the last five years. And a lot of folks we know are happy to heap the blame on those six ad agencies.

"They don't know what they're doing!"

"They're full of people with no appreciation for what it takes to create effective advertising!"

Really?

Seems unlikely.

It seems there's a problem, and it isn't necessarily with the six agencies that got fired. It's more likely with a demanding, unmanageable employer who can't get out of his own way and let the magic happen.

So, when you see lousy brand advertising and you can't figure out who the hell thought of that and why they ever thought it would work, blaming the advertising agency is easy.

And it may even be an accurate assessment.

But the blame may really lie with the client.

So, don't always shoot the messenger.

Next question: Can the good stuff, the branding that works, be pulled into your direct response advertising? Answer: Of course it can—and should.

Moreover, when you see direct response advertising for a really, really big brand, here's a virtual guarantee: the client is really smart—which means he gets out of the agency's way—and the agency really knows what they're doing.

Integrating potent brand with evocative DR is a priceless skill. It means the difference between just asking for a response and actually giving people an emotional reason to respond.

One of the simplest, most high-profile examples of this was the Denny's free Grand Slam breakfast. For a couple of years, it was advertised in the Super Bowl for the following Tuesday. Show up at Denny's between 6 a.m. and 2 p.m., and your breakfast is on the house.

This is a solid brand (America's diner), an exciting offer (a free meal), and a simple call to action (be there between 6 a.m. and 2 p.m.).

In a million years, would you ever actually think of that as DR advertising?

Probably not.

The notion of DR as so many of us understand it is practically invisible in this promotion.

But that's exactly what it is: DR.

And it may be one of the most wildly successful direct response advertisements of all time.

Moreover, the branding is a key component of this effort.

This is "America's Diner" feeding its people. Americans all over America. If Denny's didn't have a solid brand, this wouldn't work.

Since people know who Denny's is, since Denny's has spent years and untold amounts of money promoting the Grand Slam Breakfast, giving it away is a no brainer.

And the effort is also highly profitable.

Forgetting the fact that anyone who gets that free breakfast is probably also going to want a beverage (probably the most profitable section of the menu), the millions of dollars in free advertising (TV news coverage and word of mouth) is going to pay off in a big way. And, of course, they're counting on a certain percentage of repeat business from those freebie customers. Ultimately, this is all an effort to help Denny's be top-of-mind for hungry diners.

WHAT ABOUT THOSE OF US WHO AREN'T AS BIG AS DENNY'S?

Here's a little story about a small plumbing company in one of America's most average cities.

The owner of a small advertising agency went to see a demonstration of a special survey and software package that measures top of mind awareness for local businesses.

The agency owner was intrigued when the gentleman demonstrating the software happened to pick plumbers as the category for the demonstration.

And who do you think the #1 top of mind plumbing service in town was?

If you guessed Roto-Rooter, you're absolutely right.

But…

What was much more impressive was the #2 plumbing service for top of mind awareness.

It was the agency owner's client.

Years earlier, Blaine had helped this man create a branding campaign for the plumber. Because of that solid and indelible brand image, coupled with some savvy direct response advertising incorporating the brand, this plumber is dominant over every one of his local competitors.

He became the 900-pound gorilla of plumbing in town—and eventually attracted venture capital investment to expand—because he was branded well.

The only company he lost to was a behemoth of a national brand whose specialty is opening drains—a national brand whose name is probably on the lips of every adult and many children in this country when it comes time to deal with clogs.

But the bottom line is: one small local company, who uses primarily direct response advertising (and radio to boot), thrashed the competition—all because his solid brand made a clear connection to his audience. They liked him, felt like they knew him, and he became a friend.

With all other things being equal, the company with the strongest brand will win the direct response war over the company with no brand.

And that's a swell reason to brand your DR.

YEAH, WELL. I DO SOCIAL MEDIA. I DON'T NEED BRAND.

Ah. Yes. Another anti-branding bugaboo.

This one is perpetrated by certain practitioners of everyone's favorite new media darling, social media marketing.

Have you ever heard of anyone making millions through social media?

You probably have.

It would also be the exception to the rule.

The vast majority of people who are using social media make nothing.

That's because they aren't trying to. Social media is millions and millions of voices hollering into the blogosphere and the twitterverse and whatever other 'sphere' or 'verse' is inhabited by Facebook, FriendFeed, Jaiku, Ping, Plaxo, Sokule, etc., etc., so on and so on, ad infinitum.

Having a voice in social media is highly unprofitable because social media isn't a model built on making profits.

It's a model built on chaos.

If you have a business, and you want your social media efforts to pay off, it requires understanding that chaos and bringing to it a modicum of order.

And one way you bring order is by starting with a strong brand.

There are plenty of iconic national brands that have figured out how to use social media. (And plenty of others who haven't.)

Old Spice, the heritage and fuddy-duddy old brand remade as new and hip for the 21st century is just one example.

Who hasn't seen "I'm The Man Your Man Could Smell Like"? That campaign, launched in the Super Bowl, has flourished in social media in extraordinary ways. (And if you refuse to believe that YouTube is social media, you're in for a rude awakening.) As of this writing, the Old Spice Facebook page has almost 1.5 million fans. The number of views on their YouTube channel is approaching a quarter of a billion (yes, billion with a "B"). Their first Super Bowl commercial alone has 33 million views on YouTube.

That's a whole lot of people paying attention to a brand of men's deodorant.

But let's forget such obvious examples of multi-million or -billion dollar marketing for nationally known packaged goods.

Instead, let's focus on a broke nobody whose use of branded social media became a multi-million dollar concern.

(Note: if you're offended by profanity, know that the text is about to go all PG-13 on you. You may skip over it if you wish, but that would be unfortunate. We're all adults here. If you can pack away your preconceptions and stay with the program, you'll be glad you did.)

That broke nobody, whose name you probably still don't know despite his extraordinary success, is Justin Halpern.

At 29, Justin was a failed screenwriter who left Hollywood and moved back in with his father in San Diego.

Apparently, Justin's father is nuts. In a good way.

And Justin has written down some of the nutty and incredibly profane things his father says.

In August 2009, Justin channeled these profanity-laced gems of twisted parental wisdom into a Twitter feed.

You may have heard of that feed.

It's called @shitmydadsays.

In a couple of weeks, Justin had over 100,000 Twitter followers.

By October, he had a book deal with Harper Collins.

By November, he had over a million followers and a network sitcom deal with Warner Brothers for *$#*! My Dad Says* (pronounced "Bleep My Dad Says") starring William Shatner.

The book topped the New York Times bestseller list.

The sitcom ran for a season and was ultimately canceled by CBS, probably because there was no way to translate the genius of his dad's wisdom into a broadcast network sitcom without the foul-mouthed component of it.

But let's look for a moment at what Justin accomplished.

He set out to create a Twitter feed called @shitmydadsays.

In that Twitter feed, he offered exactly one element: crazy shit his dad says.

He could have been @justinhalpern and tweeted all kinds of funny stuff—including crazy things his dad says—and been no different than another of the millions of social media voices that have little to no recognition.

He would have been an unbranded member of the masses.

Instead, Justin Halpern threw vanity aside (after all it was not about him) and created an indelible, unmistakable social media brand.

That's right: @shitmydadsays is a brand.

It is designed to make people feel something very specific.

There is no mystery about what people are going to get when they go there. And fulfilling a brand's expectations is a key to its ultimate success. You've told folks, whether implicitly or explicitly, how they're going to feel. Then, you make them feel that way, every time. They are happy. People like when a promise is fulfilled. It's comforting and reassuring. It makes you a dependable source. Any person who's ever worked in advertising will tell you even the best marketing efforts can only get the public to try your product once. It's then up to the product to fulfill the advertising's expectations.

And Justin Halpern's social media brand fulfilled the expectation. It was strong enough that some of the strongest brands in traditional media decided to take a chance on it with investments totaling in the millions of dollars: Harper Collins, Warner Brothers and CBS all lined up to spend money on it. Even William Shatner. (Although he probably didn't invest any money, he did invest his brand. Yes, William Shatner is also a brand. More on that later.)

If you are driven to market your business through social media channels, guess what: you NEED a brand.

You can't just go plop your random thoughts onto a Facebook page or into the twitstream and expect it to pay off.

This is not *Field of Dreams*. If you build it, they will come *only* if you connect with them. You're competing with hundreds of millions of other voices out there in the cyber field. And might we hazard to point out that when Kevin Costner "built it," what he built was a distinct and specific connection to a poetic childhood innocence of the American psyche—creating a deeply profound and evocative reason for people to come.

He didn't build just anything. He built a de facto brand.

He didn't just plow under his corn and slap up some random, ill-considered, multi-use sporting facility for soccer, football, lacrosse and hurling in order to appeal to as many different sports fans as possible. He built one thing: a baseball diamond, a place with deep connections to people and the past. He created something that made people feel something specific. THAT is why people came. (And yes: It's also only a movie. But there's a reason why, after they made the movie, people came, and the American Film Institute has it on its "Ten Top Ten" list…)

As a business, people need to know unmistakably who you are and why you're there, and they need to feel something about your brand.

Yes, there's that word again: *feel.*

Emotion is an unmistakable key to success in marketing.

If people don't feel something about you, they won't care.

If they don't care, they won't buy.

THE BIG, SCARY TRUTH ABOUT BRAND

We're going to say it again: brand is the one way you want people to feel about your business.

And this is enormously scary to some people. The mere idea of commitment and feelings is mortifying—let alone actually committing and inspiring feelings.

We did once have to suggest to a client that maybe we weren't the right choice for branding his business. The further along the road to brand commitment we got, the more he began to flail.

Long email essays began coming about why the proposed direction—which had originally met with gleeful approval—wasn't appropriate, and he offered desperate and ham-fisted analyses of the many things that really needed to be said.

He kept trying to drag the branding effort away from brand and back into the morass from which it had emerged.

And understand, when we create a brand, we do it with the full involvement of the client. To shamelessly paraphrase Shakespeare, it's as if the mirror were held up to the client's nature. In this case, we were showing this client various different yet honest reflections of his personality.

And the more he saw, the more uncomfortable he became.

He was a perfectly nice person. But he'd been flailing in so many different directions with his attempts to brand himself for so long he was terrified of committing to any one thing.

All he could do was come up with excuses for why nothing was right.

Then, he decided that what he wanted out of a brand was to be recognized as an intellectual who was an embodiment of compassion, but would have the kind of popularity of a dynamic and edgy TV personality whose intellect and compassion were never part of the brand.

Really?

A dynamic and edgy, compassionate intellectual?

That's a pretty tall order for a brand.

Nonetheless, it would be possible to create such a brand with someone who wasn't mortified by the entire process of defining and committing to something.

When we offered this man the chance to bail, he leapt at it. And as far as we know, he still hasn't moved forward with anything.

All this to say: doing this is scary.

It requires three things: courage, honesty and commitment.

And if you're willing to go out on that three-branched tree limb of brand, you're going to find something: while it might appear to be flimsy, it's actually quite strong. It's a good place to be. While your competitors are duking it out in the muddy earth around the trunk of the tree, trying to climb atop one another in attempts to dominate, you get to stand above it all and look down, secure in the knowledge that you have something they never will.

You have a brand.

IGNITION POINTS

- There are many definitions of brand, most of which have nothing to do with brand.
- Brand is the ONE way customers should feel about your business.
- Branding a business is not the same thing as running brand advertising for a business—and branding must come first.
- Two of the biggest stumbling blocks to creating good branding are fear & ego.
- Fear says, you have to stand for more than one thing or you'll lose people. Wrong.
- Ego says, you can stand for more than one thing because you're special. Wrong.
- If a brand is properly defined, it's difficult to NOT feel something about it.

- There are times when nervousness about your brand indicates that the brand is done well.
- Good branding can make direct response advertising even more powerful.
- Good branding is vital if you want to stand out in social media.
- The idea of committing to a brand can be frightening, but the courage to commit to an honest brand is key.
- Going against your own brand can be death. Decide what you stand for and don't let fear stop you from standing for it.
- Worry not about your brand being all things to all people. Mattering a lot to some is more profitable then meaning little to a lot.

FIRESTARTER

Consider three brands that you truly admire, brands that stick with you and get under your skin. They can be big national brands, or small local businesses. The only requirement is that they stick with you and make you feel something. Analyze these brands. What is it that they mean to you? Why do they affect you? What do they leave you with before, during and after the purchase?

Chapter 3

THE SHINING BRAND ON THE HILL

Maybe apologies are in order.

We did, after all, rip off one of the strongest brands of the 20th century for the title of this chapter. Love him or hate him, there was probably no stronger brand for the US presidency in the 20th century than Ronald Reagan.

It's impossible to have felt ambivalent about Ronald Reagan—a demonstration that a good brand is indeed polarizing. And Reagan's America as a "shining city on the hill whose beacon light guides freedom-loving people everywhere" is indeed a brand-driven sentiment. It would make no sense coming from a man like Fidel Castro or Muammar Gaddafi or Hugo Chavez.

Whether you're selling political candidates or popover mix, a good brand makes people feel something and informs all of the marketing to follow. (Face it: it's impossible to feel Jiffy popover mix is anything but quick and easy.)

Here now, some glowing examples of strong brand that have followed us into this century from the last one. They've defined their respective brands very clearly and all of their marketing has always been informed by the brand direction. In most cases, they have never strayed. (Once in a while, things happen. Everyone makes mistakes.)

IT'S A HAP-HAP-HAPPY PLACE

Ever stop to wonder why McDonald's almost always wins the fast food burger wars against the other hamburger franchise behemoth, Burger King?

And isn't this especially interesting when you consider that you don't really need a taste test to know that a Burger King Whopper tastes better than a Big Mac?

McDonald's supremacy is rooted in a simple fact about their brand.

The McDonald's brand makes you feel something.

Long ago, McDonald's somehow figured out that they weren't selling hamburgers. They were selling a feeling.

And that feeling is of McDonald's as a happy place to buy a hamburger.

That's not to say McDonald's could make this brand work if they didn't have a good product. They couldn't. They have a product people like and the quality is consistent. But it is far from the best hamburger in the world.

What it is by far is the happiest hamburger in the world.

Look at who sells it: a clown.

Look how the kids' hamburger comes: in a Happy Meal.

Look at their advertising: the campaign as of this writing is "I'm Lovin' it."

Which is the successor of, "We love to see you smile."

Which is predated by campaigns like, "Nobody makes your day like McDonald's can," "It's a good time for the great taste of McDonald's," and "Food, folks and fun."

Even when the advertising wasn't quite so happy-centric, it was something else equally important.

"Your kind of place."

"We do it all for you."

"You deserve a break today."

That's right, the brand—whether it's wearing its happy on its sleeve or not—is always about the single most important person in the branding equation: you, the customer.

Now, we're going to admit here that Burger King is no slouch of a company. It's not as big or as old as McDonald's. But it certainly is a financial powerhouse, worth billions of dollars.

You'll also find that what's missing in the Burger King brand is something enormously important: you. Moreover, their brand seems largely predicated on the flame-broiled Whopper.

Burger King is selling a burger…clinically. It's flame-broiled. When Carl's Jr. sells a burger, they do it with juice unapologetically dripping down some guy's face as he blocks out the world to make love to his sandwich.

Sure, the departures from selling Whoppers are frequent and variable in their success.

But at its core, that is still what the brand seems predicated on: a flame-broiled patty.

It's difficult to feel much about a flame-broiled patty.

Burger King is a tiled room where one finds a flame-broiled Whopper.

McDonald's is a happy place.

McDonald's always makes you feel something.

Now, we are hardly going to suggest that McDonald's always gets it right. They have created some spectacular failures.

One thing that we have to recognize with the happy, you-centric McDonald's brand is that the core customer is undoubtedly your child. Their ability to market to children is one of the keys to their success. Take the kids to Mickey D's, plug them into a Happy Meal, and everything will be just fine for at least 20 minutes.

So, recognizing this fact (which seems painfully obvious once it's pointed out to you), how on earth did the Arch Deluxe ever happen?

Not that there was anything wrong with the sandwich. It was actually a pretty good burger, as fast food goes.

The problem was the advertising.

A $100 million ad campaign centered on images of children making faces at this burger. It was, after all, a sandwich targeted at adults. It was an attempt to lure grown ups into their stores for a better food experience.

Accordingly, here's what a parent saw driving down the road: a giant billboard with two golden arches on it, and images of several children looking disgusted.

That was the core of the advertising campaign.

When your brand is about happy, and parents use your business to engage their children, how successful are you going to be when your advertising starts emphasizing unhappy children?

Intellectually, it all makes perfect sense. "Hey, we can get more grown ups in here if we sell a better product."

But customers don't engage with brands on an intellectual level.

And in this case, the result was one of the most expensive flops in the history of modern American marketing.

Nice that McDonald's can engage in such an expensive flop so the rest of us can sit back and Monday-morning quarterback it as a way to understand brand.

A brief look at some other successful burger brands who vie for a piece of Mickey D's pie also shows how savvy marketers will understand the emotional component of brand and the selling of an experience rather than a sandwich.

One of the upstarts in the burger wars is the aforementioned Hardee's/Carl's Jr. (The name you know it under depends upon which market you happen to reside in.) They've done a brilliant job of appealing to a younger, male demographic with their in-your-face burger decadence. For example: using Paris Hilton in a bathing suit soaping up a Bentley before taking a bite of a burger ("That's hot"); Sir Mix-A-Lot rapping about "Flat Buns" to promote a patty melt product; or simply showing young, desirable adults engaged in burger reverie ("Don't bother me, I'm eating" and "If it doesn't get all over the place, it doesn't belong in your face"). They've gone out of their way to position themselves in a completely different world than McDonald's. Whereas

McDonald's is the happy place that appeals to Mom for her kids, Carl's Jr. and Hardee's try very specifically to appeal to a market with a prurient interest in excess. They make the burger eating experience an over-the-top, decadent moment. You feel that if you don't take the time to shut out the world and bathe in your burger, your experience is somehow less than.

Arguably, like Burger King, Carl's Jr. focuses on the burger—but not as an object. They focus on an experience that encourages strong feelings, particularly with young men. Young men who, even if they don't get the girl, can at least have a private moment with…well, a burger.

Wendy's, on the other hand, tries to play their "old fashioned hamburgers" card in various ways. The brand is perhaps best embodied by the late Dave Thomas, the company's founder. A seemingly shy, gee-whiz kinda guy, Dave Thomas was Wendy's spokesperson for years. If there was ever an example of how a brand starts at the top, this would be it.

Since Thomas's passing, Wendy's has continued to emphasize an old-fashioned quality and value persona. As of this writing, they've spent a couple of years pushing the idea that "You know when it's real." In some respects, this goes back to the whole challenge with Burger King: they're selling the food rather than the experience. Accordingly, it could be argued that Wendy's is a flawed brand.

But what Burger King and Wendy's both demonstrate is an important component to the entire brand challenge: commitment.

Even if their brands are flawed in that they've harnessed a food item rather than the experience, they are committed. And commitment to a brand is half the battle. McDonald's, Burger King, Wendy's, and Hardee's/Carl's Jr. are the nation's four largest fast food outlets in that order.

They didn't get that way by being wishy-washy in their brand commitment. They got that way by setting a course and staying true to it.

Commitment and consistency are key.

A big part of building a brand is building relationships. If you keep changing your persona, no one knows what you stand for. What's worse, if you keep flipping, they may not believe you at all.

Patience is also key. Good brands are not necessarily born overnight. Consider this: McDonald's, despite wild success since their founding in 1940, has not always been a happy place.

It was born as a speedy place.

The McDonald's mascot in 1948 was not Ronald McDonald, but Speedee, a little guy in a chef's hat who represented the Speedee Service System. Essentially, McDonald's introduced the model for the modern fast food restaurant as America was rebounding from World War II. It makes you wonder where everyone was in such a hurry to get to in 1948 that they had to get their food so speedily. But just understand this: discovering brand is often an evolutionary process. Yes, once in a while it will appear fully-formed like Athena bursting forth, grown and armored, from the head of Zeus.

But we don't live in a Greek myth.

We live in a world glutted with brands—both good and bad.

Solid relationships take time. Consider your current friends. Let's call one of them Fred. How long did it take to feel like Fred was the kind of friend with whom you could just pick up the phone and say, "What are you up to?" How much longer until you felt like you could really trust Fred? Probably not overnight. And if every time you met, Fred behaved differently in an effort to win you over, how long would it take for you to say, "See ya. I'm outta here." Making friends—and building a brand relationship—happens in its own time. If you commit.

FEEL THE LOW-COST AIRLINE LUV

You are now free to move about the country.

That's one of the sentiments recently being offered by "everyone's favorite airline," Southwest.

While calling it everyone's favorite airline might seem like a joke, a recent air traveler survey put Southwest at the top of the heap for customer satisfaction. (Delta was recognized by travelers as "the meanest" airline.)

Southwest makes a very sincere effort to share the "Luv." (If you've ever wondered why "Luv," it has to do with Southwest's history at Love Field in Texas. Special interests made it very difficult for Southwest to do business there, an airport where they were dominant, and LUV is Southwest's ticker symbol on the New York Stock Exchange.)

In their book *Made To Stick*, Chip & Dan Heath offer a very telling story about Herb Kelleher, the former CEO and one of the founders of Southwest. Essentially, the story is this: Herb Kelleher can teach you everything you need to know about running the company in 10 seconds.

Ready?

"We are the low-cost airline."

That's it.

Every business decision at Southwest is ostensibly tied to that simple directive.

What that sentiment doesn't capture, though, is an intense focus on servitude.

Southwest is an intensely customer-focused operation.

They not only make sure everything costs less; they also make sure that the customer experience is as good as it can possibly be in spite of the low-cost directive.

And note: we use the word "good" to describe the experience. Not "elevated." There's a big difference. What's good for the Southwest cattle-call would not be good for Virgin Upper Class. But in a category that is always pricey, Southwest's commitment to good service for less money means not only that you're free to move about the country, but Southwest is free to act completely differently from any other airline.

It's reflected in the attitude of the website.

It's reflected on the almost summer camp-like atmosphere onboard the planes, when flight attendants sing songs over the PA or offer their own jokey versions of the emergency announcements.

It's reflected in the advertising, where they drive home points like how easy it is to fly without the red-tape restrictions of other airlines.

It's even in their brand's color palette: happy, primary colors. Like crayons for adults.

And ultimately, it's reflected in consumer surveys that call Southwest the nicest airline to fly.

They keep prices low, and they do everything they can for you.

Contrast that with other, higher-end airline advertising, such as the commercials that show first-class passengers being doted on by women who put the "tend" in "flight attendant."

Or the decidedly business-traveler targeted commercials United ran some years back, with an animated scenario of an international business warrior slaying dragons in the Far East before returning home to his sleeping children in a Manhattan townhouse; or the high-powered businesswoman jetting off to present a PowerPoint in a foreign country—but not before slipping her heart into the coat pocket of her lover who bids her farewell in the airport. This is a brand that was targeted at the business traveler, which seems somehow vaguely consistent with its 1920s roots as an airmail carrier that began buying other airmail carriers. United has always been about business. (Brand vs. social media footnote: United received quite a black eye when a musician flying to Nebraska for a concert witnessed baggage handlers on the ground in Chicago throwing his guitar case. He subsequently discovered the guitar was broken. Throughout the claims process, he was given the endless runaround by United's customer service department. He finally made good on a threat to write three songs and produce music videos about the experience. He instantly gained international attention with the first of the three music videos, entitled "United Breaks Guitars." It has over 10 million views after a year on YouTube. The United brand suffered a serious blow because of this, and its disappearance into a merger with Continental might be fortuitous.)

Then, there's one of the truly extraordinarily lofty brands in aviation history that died such an untimely, ignominious death back in the early 1990s: Eastern Air Lines, The Wings of Man. (A lofty ad campaign for an airline notably run by World War I flying ace Eddie Rickenbacker and later astronaut Frank Borman—and a brilliant campaign created by one of the biggest of the big and ostensibly "know-nothing" ad agencies of all time, Young & Rubicam.) This is a brand that also began as an airmail carrier, but which has intense roots in aviation history. With men like Rickenbacker and Borman as the face of the company, there was always an intrinsic link to the spirit of flight. In the mid 1980s, Eastern was unable to keep up with competition from cut-rate carriers and was sold to Texas Air and Frank Lorenzo, effectively destroying what was left of the brand in a steady decline at the hands of one of *Time* Magazine's 10 "worst bosses of the century." No brand can survive at the hands of a corporate raider determined to decimate the business.

And, of course, in a classic case of disconnect between brand and customer experience, there's Delta's recent "Keep Climbing" brand campaign. Based on the 2011 Airline Quality Rating Report conducted jointly by professors from Wichita State and Purdue Universities, Delta is perceived by passengers as the nation's "meanest" airline. This unfortunate position was not helped by a 2011 social media-fueled scandal where US troops returning from the Middle East were charged thousands of dollars in extra baggage fees. At this writing, Delta's ads have talked about things like "having the passenger's back" and "building not just a bigger airline" since they acquired Northwest "but a better one." They are very artfully crafted messages that give a sense of history and immensity and tradition. But apparently, the customer experience on the ground and in the air isn't matching up with the professed brand identity. As an airline that began as a crop dusting operation in the 1920s, it seems that there's never really been a truly genuine and consistent brand identity.

As Honey likes to say, you can't fool the people for long. Your brand has to be honest. That's not to say Delta is intentionally trying to fool travelers. But there is a serious disconnect between what their ad agency is advertising and what their employees are delivering. (Know that we say this as frequent Delta customers who have never experienced the trials other passengers have apparently faced. We like Delta.)

Southwest is and always has been "the low-cost airline" with an intense focus on customer experience. It's an indelible brand, and there's a reason why it's always been healthy, even in the face of some unfortunate episodes (e.g., the aluminum skin of one of its 737s shearing off in flight).

With Southwest Airlines, you are indeed free to move about the country with a brand you understand and enjoy. They live up to their promise. More importantly, they don't promise what they choose not to deliver. It's difficult to say that about any other airline.

HOW DRIVEN ARE YOU?

Back in 2006, there was a news story about BMW and how they were going to change their 31-year old position of The Ultimate Driving Machine.

This story was met with quite an outcry.

People were beside themselves that BMW would do such a thing.

After all, this was the position that had helped carry the company from sales of around 15,000 units in 1974 to over a quarter of a million units in 2005.

Ostensibly, they were going to replace "The Ultimate Driving Machine" with "A Company of Ideas."

As you probably realize, this never happened. BMW was and as of this writing remains The Ultimate Driving Machine.

Moreover, there's an unsubstantiated rumor that the story was a total fabrication. That BMW never had any plans to change their position. The story is alleged to have been created by a savvy marketing guy as a PR stunt to get people talking about BMW.

There's no way to prove it.

But it seems to make sense.

After all, why would BMW abandon an established brand that has been so outrageously successful and has shown no evidence of slowing down?

Automotive is a category that has always garnered fierce brand loyalty. People are often not just (fill in the blank) auto brand owners; they are (fill in the blank) auto brand families.

The bottom line for The Ultimate Driving Machine is that BMW owns the idea of driving. It owns precision. It owns road-hugging, fast-accelerating, Teutonic austerity.

It also owns a market populated by aggressive A-type overachievers (and those who wish they were). A marketing executive at BMW was once quoted as saying they were a "progressive, go get 'em company," which is an interesting quote. That attitude is reflected in all of their marketing and is characteristic of the core BMW customer. There is certainly no automobile brand that makes anyone feel quite as significant as BMW. They own the idea of precision driving and everything that goes with it, and the brand makes the core customer feel as important as he believes he is.

WHO LEAVES THE LIGHT ON FOR YA?

The one national motel chain that is top of mind for an inexpensive room is undoubtedly Motel 6. For over a quarter century, this iconic motelier has capitalized on Tom Bodett's folksy voice and an equally folksy piece of violin music to convey exactly what they are: the budget motel that cares.

(**SIDEBAR**: Neither that voice nor that music on their own is the Motel 6 brand. They are Motel 6 brand *triggers*. They remind you who's talking to you. By committing to these elements in all of its marketing, Motel 6 triggers your recognition of its brand quickly and efficiently. But by themselves, they are not the brand.)

What's interesting is that the core idea, the unique selling proposition, of Motel 6's position is not the first thing anyone thinks of: it claims the lowest priced room of any national motel chain.

But what people always remember is "We'll leave the light on for you."

This is an incredibly potent and very important notion.

It lends considerable veracity to the idea that people respond to your brand emotionally.

Yes, Motel 6 is cheap. They make no bones about that.

But what everyone remembers is the emotional core of the brand. Because really, who leaves the light on for you?

Mom.

Your wife.

Your husband.

Whoever is at home when you're on the road leaves the light on for you so when you come home, you're not in the dark.

The light is left on by someone who truly cares about you.

Motel 6 could have said, "We care about you."

And that would be a hollow, empty sentiment. After all, if you have to say it, you're not proving anything and are making the sentiment suspect. (See also: the used car salesman who says, "You can trust me.")

Motel 6 could also have said, "Open 24 hours a day." It's a fact. After all, that's why the light is on.

But facts are often cold, hard and are unable to pass what Blaine calls "The So What Test." The human response these facts generate—if they generate any response at all—is, "So what?"

In the case of Motel 6, its highly successful brand is about making an emotional connection. It goes way beyond "So what?"

Motel 6 originally began as a $6 a night motel started by a couple of Southern California contractors in 1962. The plan was to offer an ever-more-mobile America an alternative to Holiday Inn and the other, pricier chains of the day.

The "We'll leave the light on for you" branding campaign was created by The Richards Group of Dallas back in the mid 1980s. It came at a time when there was a glut of empty motel rooms on the market. When the ad campaign finally hit, it reversed a huge occupancy void practically overnight.

Everything about the Tom Bodett campaign is very deliberate and calculated. There's a story that the creative director at The Richards Group called up Tom Bodett who was a carpenter in Alaska who occasionally did commentary on NPR. Apparently, Tom Bodett asked why they wanted his voice.

The creative director is reputed to have said, "Because you sound like a guy who would stay at Motel 6."

A lofty sounding gentleman with a British accent would be outside of the Motel 6 brand. You wouldn't hire a Prince Charles impersonator to voice Motel 6 commercials. Once you are clear on your brand, such style choices become much easier and more cohesive.

The Motel 6 advertising sounds right, it says the right things, it's very much calculated to resonate on an emotional level with the core customer.

Moreover, like any of the other brands being discussed here, it's completely honest. It delivers exactly on the promise of the brand. You go to Motel 6 and you get a clean, no-frills room.

And when you pull up to that Motel 6 after dark, weary from the road and wishing you were home, the light is on for you.

BUILDING ANYTHING OF VALUE?

There's been a recent emergence of new branding at, of all places, The Home Depot. Granted, the company is more or less the same as it ever was. But the branding campaign they've been running as of this writing seems to have hit the nail on the head in the way that previous campaigns haven't.

Over the last couple of decades, The Home Depot brand campaigns have said things like, "You can do it. We can help." Which, honestly, implies that The Home Depot is a place for the helpless. The campaign for "The Home Depot, Low prices are just the beginning," attempts to own the idea of low prices. Unfortunately, low prices don't necessarily connote value and often are code for low quality. The idea of "When you're at The Home Depot, You'll feel right at home" is a disconnect that sounds more like it's trying to compete with Motel 6. And "The Home Depot: First in Home Improvement!" is a declaration of supremacy without anything to really back it up. BMW's Ultimate Driving Machine might be a cocky, self-satisfied position—but the brand follows through. BMW is a hell of a car. Is Home Depot really first in home improvement in any meaningful way?

We would posit that now, maybe it is—even though there are still a lot of folks who get on a soap box and tell you why they will drive past Home Depot to go to Lowe's.

But in our minds, Home Depot's brand is stronger. "More saving. More doing." That's now "the power of The Home Depot." It might seem like a small step from some of the aforementioned branding campaigns. But something about this particular position brings with it a potency that none of the others really do. In a time of economic downturn, and in a time when Home Depot has been experiencing declines, the idea of spending less yet actually doing more brings with it an optimism that people could really use.

Yes, you really can have the power to do more with less, and the Home Depot is the place to get that power.

Interestingly, at least in our market, Home Depot runs a lot of radio advertising specifically targeted at contractors. At a time when contractors are definitely experiencing challenges, the idea of doing more with less seems like a really salient notion. But what these ads do (for our money) is something significant as far as the consumer is concerned: it makes The Home Depot sound like a place truly worthy of their business. After all, if it's good enough for contractors, it should certainly be good enough for my DIY projects.

We all know who and what The Home Depot is. It's a big box home improvement store where many tend to shop by default. But with the "more saving, more doing" campaign, it seems to have become a brand that actually empowers us to get stuff done without taking on a second mortgage.

FOR MORE THAN JUST HOOKING UP

The immediacy and superficiality of the internet seems to have done a lot to fuel immediate, superficial relationships. The notion of guys and gals "hooking up" for casual, uncommitted relationships has paralleled the rise of a casual, uncommitted medium.

That said, the internet is also a tool that is quite powerful in its ability to effect serious change. And no, we're not talking about fueling revolutions in the Middle East. We're talking about the internet's most famous and preeminent dating website, eHarmony.

Dedicated to creating matches based on "the deepest levels of compatibility," eHarmony is a potent brand. It fuels that brand in its advertising in two ways: one, through the presence of its gentlemanly founder, Dr. Neil Clark Warren (who has been reappearing in the advertising after a hiatus); and two, through the glowing testimonials of real people who met on eHarmony.

One of the things that is really interesting about the eHarmony people is that so often, they are absolutely NOT glamorous. They are so real, it's staggering. They're often not the prettiest of people. Many are overweight, they don't have impossibly white teeth, they're not wearing the latest fashions, and their last trip to the gym was, well, you know. But, what makes them attractive is the genuine stories they tell and the real emotions behind them. And what they all have in common is big smiles and glowing praise for eHarmony and the relationship they found there. Key word: "smiles."

In junior high, Honey had a teacher who gave a slide show of photos he took while in Morocco. The people in the photos looked nothing like anyone this class had ever seen. The faces were weathered, and many of these people were missing teeth. But they were all smiling genuinely happy, honest smiles. The teacher stood in front of his class and said, "Everyone is beautiful when they smile."

And you know what?

He was right.

He knew it then, and the talented folks at DonatWald+Haque, who created the eHarmony advertising, know it today.

These eHarmony people are insanely Happy, Happy, Happy.

And their enthusiasm comes across load and clear. It's infectious.

You can feel it coming out of your television at you.

These people are the incarnation of the eHarmony brand, connected on the deepest levels of compatibility.

The brand promise is clearly stated: if you want a truly compatible mate, eHarmony is for you. And the brand advertising clearly proves the ability of eHarmony to deliver on that brand promise.

YOU MIGHT NOT HAVE A NATIONAL OR MULTI-NATIONAL COMPANY

Accordingly, you might reason that you don't need a brand. You might also reason that, since you're a sole proprietor rather than a company with employees, you don't need a brand.

Either way, we still maintain that having a brand is now more important than ever. In an ever-fragmented communication landscape with ever-more marketing messages, you need to focus your brand more than ever.

We're also going to prove that you don't need to be a big company. We're going to provide irrevocable evidence that even a single individual benefits from brand.

IGNITION POINTS

- A good brand is often polarizing.
- McDonald's focuses not on a sandwich, but on the McDonald's experience—more attractive for Mom than a decadent burger brand like Carl's Jr. or Hardees.
- Southwest Airlines puts the "luv" in low cost air travel—but definitely makes high-end business travelers want to stay away.
- The eHarmony brand is great for people interested in having a committed relationship, but is unlikely to appeal to people who are interested in simply "hooking up."
- In an increasingly fragmented media environment, where more and more people are clamoring for your customer's attention, having a strong and perhaps polarizing brand is more important than ever.

FIRESTARTER

Consider three brands that you don't like at all—in fact, consider three brands that you hate. Do you hate them because they are executed badly—or do you hate them because they create a feeling that is outside of your zone as a consumer?

Chapter 4

THE SOUND OF A ONE-MAN BRAND LAUGHING ALL THE WAY TO THE BANK

Branding is not just for advertising.

Branding is for any business that wants to make a mark. And here now, the evidence to prove it.

Comedians.

If you are or have ever been a fan of stand-up comedy, you know that comedians are very different from one another.

But have you ever stopped for a second to think about what a comedian is and why you feel as you do about him or her?

A comedian is a business.

One person, perhaps, but a complete business.

And every successful comedian has a brand.

Never really thought of it that way, didja?

Some folks think that if you go to a comedian's home, everything is an endless laugh riot, that every room in the house is finished with at least one exposed brick wall, and there are always microphone stands and spotlights at the ready.

The reality: living with a comedian is a lot like living with anyone else.

But once a comedian goes to the stage, they shed 96% of their personality.

The remaining 4% is intensely focused on one thing: making you laugh.

And one of the ways that happens is by constructing a solid comedy brand that is identifiable and repeatable.

Each successful comedian builds a brand that makes you feel something specific.

Here now, a brief analysis of a few high-profile comedy brands.

EVERYONE'S FAVORITE HAPPY-GO-LUCKY HICK

It's difficult to be a cogent American beyond age 12 and not have had at least a passing encounter with the comedy routine, "You might be a redneck if…" (For example: "If you think the last words to The Star Spangled Banner are, 'Gentlemen, start your engines,' you might be a redneck.")

The man responsible for this insanely simple, highly profitable comedy meme is Jeff Foxworthy.

As a brand, it's safe to say Jeff Foxworthy is worth millions.

His brand is represented by *The Blue Collar Comedy Tour*, a network sitcom, a network game show, several bestselling books, a nationally syndicated radio show, five comedy CDs, the many TV specials and DVDs spawned by *The Blue Collar Comedy Tour*, and one moderately successful Christmas novelty song that briefly appeared on the Hot Country Songs chart.

This man is a redneck dynamo.

Did you know that he has a college degree from Georgia Tech, one of the top ten public universities in the nation, and used to work on mainframe computers at IBM?

Of course not.

Because it's not part of the brand.

The Jeff Foxworthy brand is a very calculated veneer of affable redneck, good-old-boy charm and well-crafted routines that do not in any way ruin that veneer.

For Jeff Foxworthy's comedy, that good old boy veneer is his brand.

Every joke he tells, every book he writes, everything in which he participates upon the public stage fits with his brand.

Being the highly-educated computer geek son of an IBM executive does not.

SIDEBAR: *The Blue Collar Comedy Tour*'s Larry the Cable Guy is truly a bit more of what his brand suggests. Larry grew up on a pig farm in Nebraska. He also went to college, and his real name is Daniel Lawrence Whitney—but you'll never hear about those two tidbits, as they don't fit with Larry's brand, either.

Jeff Foxworthy, comedian, is a brand. Jeff Foxworthy, Georgia Tech alum, computer geek, and son of Jimmy and Carole, is just another guy from Atlanta.

Picking a brand persona and focusing it, honing it, concentrating it, and distilling it into the You-Might-Be-A-Redneck-If Guy has made him a very successful commodity in the entertainment business.

Promoters and producers would have no idea what to do with an Atlanta redneck computer geek from Georgia Tech who tells jokes. Too much information.

But get rid of all the extras that send you in different directions, focus down to one resonant concept, and it's easy to figure out what to do with Mr. You Might Be A Redneck If…

What you do is cash in.

Jeff Foxworthy is a brand that's easy to understand.

The brand also lets his audience know how they're supposed to feel. "I am a redneck or somehow connected to rednecks and this guy gets me." He's taking all the mundane things about a certain lifestyle and making them special. So people feel special to be part of his club. Because while they might be rednecks, the guy in a tailored suit and Italian leather shoes is not. He can't join their club.

THROW THE DICE

Crass. Crude. Racist. Homophobic. Misogynistic.

Call him what you will. You either hate him, love him, or love to hate him. However you feel about him, Andrew Dice Clay is a distinctive and clearly defined comedy brand.

The titles of the Diceman's comedy albums and TV specials are very much in keeping with the Dice brand.

Assume The Position.

Filth.

The Mixtape That Hates You.

No Apologies.

There others that are more crude than we'd like to mention here.

And chances are, just mentioning all this makes you feel something.

Welcome to the world of a successful brand.

We're not saying we *like* the brand. We actually don't care for it at all. But many others do.

And herein lies one of the keys to a successful brand: quite often, an effective brand is polarizing.

When you make an audience truly feel something, they pay attention.

That doesn't mean they need to like it. One man's meat is another man's poison.

And while you might regard the Diceman as poison, you know he's going to have something really crass to say about his own meat.

Interestingly, Andrew Clay Silverstein grew up entertaining his family by doing impressions. As a boy drummer, he played bar mitzvahs. He did not grow up as the lurid and prurient Diceman. Creating Dice was a conscious effort to focus on his particular brand of id gone horribly wrong.

It also made him enormously successful.

And when Andrew Dice Clay, comedian, abandoned the "Dice" and tried to become Andrew Clay, actor, guess what?

His established brand was so polarizing that even when he tried to step out of the Diceman brand package and rebrand himself as an actor, it didn't take.

Special-interest groups denounced him like crazy.

And were his fans there for him? If so, there weren't anywhere near enough of them. When Andrew Clay's NBC sitcom *Bless This House* debuted in 1995, it lasted one season. When it tanked, Andrew Clay the actor went away and Andrew Dice Clay the raunchy comedian made his way back to headlining in Vegas, complete with his profane, misanthropic brand intact.

This also underscores the importance of brand expectations.

Neither his fans nor his detractors would accept the man as a straight actor.

It just wasn't the Diceman that they were promised would show up. It was some other guy. Not fulfilling your promise is disappointing, and disappointment will not win your brand any friends.

It's just as if you promised your mother a night with Jeff Foxworthy, and when you got there, the Diceman came out.

Mom would probably not be OK with that. He's not your mom's brand. Unless, of course, your mom is one strange cookie.

HOW DO YOU FEEL ABOUT THE QUEEN OF MEAN?

Lisa Lampanelli gets around. Yes, it's possible you may not have heard of her. Nonetheless, she is popular and successful as a racy, raunchy, foul-mouthed white girl who talks about things no girl is supposed to talk about. Think Don Rickles for the new millennium.

Not surprisingly, she has made a name for herself as a frequent participant in comedy roasts. She was heavily influenced by watching televised broadcasts of Dean Martin's comedy roasts when she was a kid. She's brought a dirty and dangerous wit to roasting the likes of Pamela Anderson, William Shatner, Gene Simmons, and David Hasselhoff, just to name a few.

One of her frequent topics is race—she makes many jokes about having dated black men. She also makes a lot of explicit jokes about sex.

These are traditionally taboo subjects for female comics. Women of an earlier generation would never have gotten away with that.

And Lisa Lampanelli has become widely known as The Queen of Mean.

So, what about this enormously polarizing brand differs from the Diceman?

By her own assertion, it's that she has a "warm personality" and "good intentions." Yes, that sounds like a stretch. If you see her perform, you might be shocked—but you'll also understand what she means. It's difficult to not like this woman, even when the worst possible things are coming out of her mouth. There's a decidedly different spin to her humor than to what's been called "the comedy of hate" delivered by nastier comics.

She's also not a stupid woman by any stretch. She did her undergrad work in journalism at Boston College and Syracuse University and did graduate work at Harvard. That separates her somewhat from Andrew Dice Clay and moves her more towards the Foxworthy camp.

You'll also never hear about it in her act because it's off-brand. "I did graduate work at Harvard" doesn't really jive with, "Betty White is so old that on her first game show ever, the grand prize was fire."

Rather than Dicegirl, she's Donna Rickles. She loves her audience, and they love her. The Queen of Mean is an endearment. She might not be your cup of tea, her brand might be too far off the mainstream for you to enjoy it, but you know who she is and there's no mystery about what you're going to hear when you go see her. She is a ribald, R-rated hussy with heart. If that's not for you, she's OK with that.

One last thing about Miss Lampanelli: she gets brand, big time. She knows exactly what she's doing with her brand to the point that in a show we saw, she actually discussed "her brand" on stage. (We were so proud.)

HOW BLACK IS YOUR SENSE OF HUMOR?

Are you a frustrated, neurotic, socialist curmudgeon who frequently feels pushed to the brink of sanity?

If so, you probably take some comfort in the fact that Lewis Black makes you look like a Buddhist monk.

Everyone's favorite neurotic, politically-charged New Yorker, Lewis Black has made a name for himself by appearing as though the absurdities of everyday life have pushed him to the brink of apoplexy. His highly charged rants lead to bouts of shouting and finger-shaking as he reaches his personal limits. He takes on politics, religion, trends, history, and various cultural phenomena.

And really, none of this should be surprising. A child of the '60s, this is a man who studied as a playwright at The University of North Carolina at Chapel Hill (one of the pre-eminent American schools for theater), and received an MFA from the Yale School of Drama.

These facts, of course, are not part of his brand.

"I'm the Yale-educated lunatic leftist playwright absurdist" isn't relevant to the brand. It might help explain how the brand came to be. He knows a lot about a lot. But it's not germane to the Lewis Black brand image.

Fittingly, Lewis Black's last name is very much part of his brand. His humor is often very black. And the titles of his books and recordings capitalize on both the name and the brand.

I'm Dreaming of a Black Christmas.

Nothing's Sacred.

Me of Little Faith.

Stark Raving Black.

The End of the Universe.

For anyone who is a fan of relatively gentle comedy like that of Jeff Foxworthy—a man who is a devout Christian and has performed for the Christian youth organization, Young Life—Lewis Black's name couldn't be more appropriate, and probably serves as a warning.

Lewis Black is definitely not a brand for everyone. He's focused on a city-dwelling, neurotic brand of comedy lover, overly obsessed with how the political, racial and social sky is falling.

And he's just fine with that.

KEEPING IT SQUEAKY CLEAN

Lest anyone think that our idea of well-defined brands is purely those that might be considered somehow unholy, it might be helpful at this point to swing away from the black end of the spectrum, shoot past the relatively wholesome Jeff Foxworthy, and look at the complete other end of the scale.

You might remember Victoria Jackson from her years on *Saturday Night Live*. She was the high-voiced, bubble-headed blond who was often the butt of suggestive jokes. She also was and still is a stand-up comic. Her first notable TV appearance was on *The Tonight Show* with Johnny Carson, reciting poetry while doing a handstand. This particular stunt became a signature part of her comedy routine.

And when she was hired for *Saturday Night Live,* Victoria Jackson was plugged right into the slot of Designated Airhead.

After all, it was her brand.

At one point, while doing a bit that lived up to her airhead brand, she stopped and said, "I can't do this Victoria 'airhead' thing anymore." She pulled off the blond hair, revealing a short brunette wig underneath.

She then announced that she couldn't believe how people thought she really was such an airhead. From now on, her act would be nothing but serious political commentary.

It never was, of course. She continued being true to the Victoria Jackson brand as Designated Airhead.

In her post *SNL* career, Victoria Jackson continues to entertain. She performs stand up. She has produced CDs of music for children. And since *Saturday Night Live*, both her Christian faith and conservative politics have very much become part of her brand.

She is very clearly defined in her brand identity and is definitely not a brand for everyone.

And Victoria is just fine with that.

As far as she's concerned, her brand answers to a higher power.

WHAT DOES ALL THIS HAVE TO DO WITH YOU?

A couple of things.

For one, it demonstrates the potency of a solid, well-thought-out brand in an attempt to make scads of money. After all, each of these brands has gained national attention to varying degrees. The Jeff Foxworthy brand alone is worth millions. And really, what's it predicated on? One idea. A single idea that makes his audience feel one way. Which means that even if you were to strip away all of the peripheral money-making apparatus, like network television and books and CDs, this brand could still be a money maker. All you need is the man, a room full of people, and a clearly defined brand. (The last component is the hard part.) Keep duplicating that effort, and Jeff Foxworthy would still be a cash machine. Not nearly as profitable, but profitable nonetheless.

That's because what sells is the brand.

There is no tangible product.

There is no professional service.

There are only words in the air—words that have been arranged in a way that lives up to and honors the brand.

Additionally, these comic brands serve as an example to anyone who thinks, "Well, I'm not selling packaged goods or a national franchise, and I don't have a store. I don't need a brand."

Wrong-O.

If you're a sole proprietor with a home office who offers consultation, you're in dire need of a brand.

In fact, you might be more in dire need of a brand than a much larger operation.

That's because you don't have deep pockets and an endless advertising budget and any of the other resources that a large company does.

You need a brand identity that gives you a distinct profile and makes your prospects feel something about you.

Yes, you do widget sales coaching from home. But so does that gal down the block. Now what? How are you going to talk to folks about widget sales coaching differently than she does? Are you the crass, in-your-face widget coach or the "you might be a widget seller if..." coach?

Which is the brand that represents you and appeals to your particular widget-buying audience?

One man alone in a room with a miniscule advertising budget is going to lose to another man alone in a room with a miniscule advertising budget AND a solid, recognizable, meaningful brand—a brand that makes me feel something.

And that man alone in a room with a miniscule advertising budget and a solid brand is never going to worry a multi-national competitor who does the same thing that he does.

But that multi-national competitor will lose a few potential customers to a competing, well-branded sole proprietorship.

In the world of big business brand advertising, the goal is to "move the needle." The advertisers typically expect small, incremental changes in business. A 2% uptick in sales can often be considered reason to pop the champagne corks.

If one man can take away just a few customers from a huge company, the huge company will never notice—but the one man could utterly change his own life.

A solid brand greatly improves the odds of one man alone in a room.

And finally, what these comic brands demonstrate is the power of emotion in the brand paradigm.

It is impossible to not feel something with a man as polarizing as Andrew Dice Clay. You might find him repulsive.

Go right ahead and be repulsed.

Because there is a crass, bottom-feeding audience out there that's just as happy to embrace him.

And he's all right with that.

This is a question for the prospect: whose team do you want to be on?

A woman who wants to be on Victoria Jackson's conservative Christian team likely has no interest in being on Lisa Lampanelli's profane, bawdy, sex-talk team.

And each of them is OK with that.

Note: There are going to be those of you reading this who say, I'm not OK with that. My audience is everyone. The entire world could buy my widget sales coaching. Hear this: the entire world won't buy your widget sales coaching. And if you try to get them all, all you'll get is no one. That's a promise from us to you. But be special to a clearly defined target group, and you will be able to pay your bills and then some.

There's a lawyer in Los Angeles who specializes in representing drunk drivers. His brand is The DUI Top Gun Attorney. You've probably heard the line, "Friends don't let friends drive drunk." The tag line for this lawyer's brand is, "Friends don't let friends plead guilty."

His brand (understandably) offends a great many people.

And he's OK with that.

Because he doesn't want the people who are offended by it.

He wants the people who need representation for having been arrested while driving under the influence.

Yes, their infraction is inexcusable.

But they still need a lawyer to represent them.

And he's the first guy a lot of people are going to think of.

No matter what you do, your brand cannot possibly appeal to everyone.

We have a medical provider client in a rural New England community who runs radio advertising. His commercials are very honest, extemporaneous expressions of the service he provides. The brand's core target customer is Mom. And one of his commercials talks about how, as medical professionals, "We call ourselves primary care providers, but the real primary care provider is Mom. She's not educated in this. But she often knows what to do."

There were a couple of people who were deeply offended by this. They responded very vocally to the doctor's office.

So he rushed right out and changed his advertising.

Kidding.

His staff said they were sorry the listeners were offended.

And the good doctor continued right on running the advertising.

He's a homey, no-nonsense, pro-Mom kinda guy. And his phraseology apparently rubs a couple of folks the wrong way.

He's not going to change anything about that position. In fact, for anyone who IS offended by that position, we suspect he'd rather not see them in his office.

The more potent your brand, the more likely you are to offend someone.

There will inevitably be a polarizing element to your brand.

A polarized audience is paying attention.

And no matter the size of your company, whether you have many employees or you're merely one man in a room, a solid brand dramatically improves your chances of success on the stage of commerce.

One last point on the comedians as examples of solid branding: none of these folks have a logo, font, color, jingle, or any of the things typically associated with branding. Yet, they all have great brands. So good, in fact, that if someone showed you a logo for Jeff Foxworthy or the Diceman, you'd know if it was right or not.

Why?

Because you would feel it.

Therein, the power of brand.

It's not just for breakfast—or for advertising.

It's for you.

IGNITION POINTS

- Branding is not just for advertising, but for any individual who wants to have a clear, successful, high-profile presence.
- Comedians are an excellent example of branded individuals.
- Comedians are not the people you see onstage, but a concentrated persona from a sliver of their actual personality.
- Each comedian makes you feel something specific about their brand.
- Anything that doesn't feed the brand—like Jeff Foxworthy's background as a computer geek or Lisa Lampanelli's Harvard education—are left out.

- Each of these brands is wildly successful—without any of the presumed components of brand, like a font, a color or a logo.
- Each of these brands is unafraid of alienating someone who is not in the target demographic.
- It is better (see also: more profitable) to be loved by a smaller yet devoted group than just to be there, throwing yourself at the undefined masses.
- A solidly crafted brand greatly improves the odds of success for one man alone in a room.

FIRESTARTER

Think about three performers you recognize and are possibly attracted to because of the individual's brand persona. They could be comedians or musicians or actors. But chances are they represent something very specific. What is it about each of these personal brands that you can take a cue from in your branding effort? Choose one and consider what colors might best represent them. This will show how a clearly defined brand starts to help you make cohesive choices.

Chapter 5
THE POWER OF ONE

There is so, so much you want to say.

And really?

Nobody cares.

At least, not in your branding.

Sorry to have to break it to you this way.

The more you want to say about your business with your brand, the more you're going to turn off your prospects.

The more you cram in there, the more likely you are to send them into the waiting arms of a brand that says one thing and one thing only.

The simple fact is that we live in an over-communicated culture.

Under the best of circumstances, most people barely have the attention span required to focus on one thing and one thing only.

If you're trying to bombard them with too many things, how much attention can you expect them to give you?

Zip-O.

You can't make your brand about everything you do. You have to make your brand about one thing and one thing only. The power of one is key in both branding and in advertising a brand. Once you get them in, you can beguile them with everything else that's so fabulous. Right now is not the time.

HOW HUNGRY ARE YOU TO SOLVE THE PROBLEM?

A perfect example of the power and potency of One comes from the charities that feed children in foreign countries.

"There are 17 million starving children in Botswagos" might be a fact relevant to the plight of global starvation.

But it isn't a fact that anyone feels deeply about.

"Yeah, that's tragic. Speaking of starving children, is it lunchtime yet?"

But something happens when you take those 17 million starving children, and select one child's face and story from the teeming throng.

"This is Lily. She is 5 years old and lives in Botswagos. She's a lot like other 5 year old girls. She likes to play with her sock monkey, who's missing one eye. She takes care of her little brother. She also works in the fields with her mother and father, who are dirt farmers in this dry, arid country. Lily lives on the edge of starvation. She often goes for days without a proper meal. But you can help."

17 million starving children is too big, too overwhelming, and people are too powerless to do anything about it. And, unfortunately, it becomes sterile. Because you can't feel that much, you feel nothing.

But when the problem is reduced to the plight of a single child, when you give someone the option of "adopting" a kid who will write thank you notes and talk about her life, you turn the problem from unsolvable to immediately manageable. "I can do something about one small child who loves her one-eyed sock monkey and needs a meal that costs only 7 cents."

In essence, organizations like Feed The Children brand the problem one child at a time. It's what wins them friends and influences people to donate.

YOU LAUGH—OR YOU CRY

The same thing happens at the movies.

If you go to an Arnold Schwarzenegger movie, you're not going to be surprised by the body count. *Commando* tops the Schwarzenegger Body Count list with 88 corpses. In *Total Recall*, there are 77 victims. In *True Lies*, 71 actors went down to collect pay checks as dead bodies.

This doesn't surprise anyone, and chances are good you don't feel a thing for any of those dead characters.

In fact, there's a high likelihood a lot of the guys are going to cheer whenever the body count ticker adds another victim.

But in *Terms of Endearment*, there is a body count of exactly one: Debra Winger's character, Emma.

And the entire movie has been predicated on making you feel something for that woman named Emma.

So, when Emma dies, the women all cry and the men pretend not to.

That's because the one-thing-and-one-thing-only paradigm is at play.

The one character is calculated to hook you emotionally.

The one character has been designed to make you care.

And when that one character is taken from you, it stirs your emotions.

You don't care about the faceless mass of 17 million starving children in Botswagos or the 236 violently dispatched corpses in *Commando, Total Recall* and *True Lies.*

But boy, do you feel something for Lily on the Botswagos dirt farm and Emma in *Terms of Endearment.*

We can connect to the one. But, give people too many things to care about, they can focus on nothing. They simply glaze over and move on.

BRAND OF ENDEARMENT

It's all about focusing on one and only one emotional hook.

People simply do not have the ability to focus on more than one thing at a time.

When it comes to brand, that's why BMW is The Ultimate Driving Machine.

Not the Luxurious Precision Driving Machine with a Great Stereo From the Dealer Who Really Cares About Your Experience for All Your Car Buying Needs.

That latter sentiment is half loaded with irrelevant BS.

Beyond that, it simply isn't something anyone can focus on.

The actual BMW Ultimate Driving Machine brand is pithy and relevant and in your face.

And you can focus on it.

It also has emotional appeal to a certain kind of A-type mentality—people who feel superior, or who "know" they're superior, or who would really like to be superior.

It appeals to people who appreciate precision and all the really great stuff that comes with it.

It appeals to people who like going to a dealership where the salesmen bow and scrape a little.

Contrary to the jokes about BMW owners, they aren't all nasty, condescending, obnoxious yuppies with narcissistic personality disorder.

But there is just a little bit of something in every one of them that really grooves on the reality of the brand.

BUT—DOES BMW LEAVE THE HEADLIGHTS ON FOR YOU?

On the other side of the brand coin, there's Motel 6.

Motel 6 could be the Open All The Time With Clean Rooms And No Frills Because We Know You Don't Want To Spend A Lot of Money But We Care About Your Experience Budget Motel…Oh And We're Conveniently Located.

But who'd pay attention to that?

Nobody.

Before they were halfway through saying it to you, you'd be saying, "Oh, look, a Travelodge. They've got the sleepy bear. Let's stay there."

But almost everybody—even people who would never actually stay at Motel 6—can tell you that Motel 6 leaves the light on for you.

Why?

Because it's one thing.

And more than just one thing, it's one poetic thing.

Poetry is an enormously powerful tool when used correctly.

And no, poetry need not rhyme.

What is poetry, exactly? To again borrow from everyone's favorite e-source du jour, Wikipedia, poetry is "a form of literary art in which language is used for its aesthetic and evocative qualities in addition to, or in lieu of, its apparent meaning."

The key word there, in relation to Motel 6, is "evocative."

Evocative: to evoke.

To call up, summon forth, produce or provoke.

Motel 6 is, fundamentally, the Open All The Time With Clean Rooms And No Frills Because We Know You Don't Want To Spend A Lot of Money But We Care About Your Experience Budget Motel.

That 30-word nonsense sentiment also doesn't make anyone care.

It doesn't call up, summon forth, produce or provoke a damn thing.

Except, perhaps, incredulity that anyone would expect you to pay attention.

But the idea of Mom?

That makes people care.

And what does Mom have for you?

She has your old room.

It's not fancy.

But it's the place where you always knew you were welcome.

And Mom kept it clean. There was always going to be soap in the shower, clean sheets on the bed, and a clean towel on the rack.

And when Mom knew you were going to be out late, what would she always do for you?

She'd leave the light on for you.

Just like Motel 6.

The Motel 6 brand, even if people don't understand it consciously, is a brand evocative of Home.

As the book says, you never want to play cards with a man named Doc, and you never want to eat at a place called Mom's.

But is there anything wrong with getting a room at a place that sounds as good as Mom's house?

Because Mom cares.

Mom and Motel 6 leave the light on for you.

The brand says one thing and one thing only.

And as it happens, it's a very, very potent one thing.

The Ultimate Driving Machine?

Potent as well.

So why is good poetry evocative in marketing? Because it dares to sound different to the ear. Which means in a sea of advertisers who think their brand is "For all your [fill in the blank] needs," a pithy poetic thought stands out.

BMW could have easily said, "We're the best automobile you can buy."

But no.

They are The Ultimate Driving Machine.

These are brands that are both winners.

BMW has lived by their brand for over 35 years.

Motel 6 has lived by theirs for over 25 years.

And really, what's the difference, ten years here or there, once you've got a brand and it demonstrates a life of its own that attracts customers and continues building the bottom line?

RHYME TIME FOR THE BRAND OF THE CENTURY?

Since we've begun discussing poetry, let's talk about another brand that has continued its brand commitment for over 70 years—and has done so using a different kind of poetry than Motel 6.

It has used a less metaphorically loaded poetry in lieu of one that totally says the obvious—and rhymes.

To be completely fair, the company has been around for over 70 years, but the brand poetry has only been around for just over 50 years.

It's also a virtual guarantee that you know the words to the rhyme.

Ready?

"Call Roto-Rooter, that's the name, and away go troubles down the drain."

Do you have any idea how many Roto-Rooter guys are also plumbers?

Probably every single one of them.

Do you ever hear a Roto-Rooter guy advertising general plumbing services?

Heck no!

Why?

Because Roto-Rooter has a lock on the one-thing-and-one-thing-only paradigm. They KNOW where the money is.

When a woman is standing ankle-deep in filthy water, the first name on her lips is Roto-Rooter.

That Roto-Rooter guy comes in and saves the day, quickly and easily.

THEN, he lets his customer know should she ever need plumbing service of any description, he's there for her.

He might even have another listing under general plumbing services.

But the king of brand in plumbing is and always will be Roto-Rooter.

Because, "Call Roto-Rooter, that's the name, and away go troubles down the drain."

One thing and one thing only, driven home by a relentlessly simple and repetitive jingle. It's not high poetry.

It's closer to doggerel.

It will never win any creativity awards.

But boy, does it work like magic.

If there's such a thing as lowbrow genius, the Roto-Rooter jingle is it.

And again, once you hook them with your one poetic clog-removing thing and you're embedded in their hearts and minds, you can take your face time with them to let them in on the other plumbing-related things they're sure to love about you.

THIS IS, AFTER ALL, NOT A CONTEST ABOUT ART

It's a contest to get more customers.

It also takes place in a marketplace increasingly crowded with businesses clamoring for the same customers you are.

So what's your one point of difference?

Why are people going to care about it?

And how are you going to state it to make people care?

Doing this all with a degree of artistry is nice.

But a degree of clarity is essential.

"We'll leave the light on for you" is a nicely phrased sentiment that is clear, timeless, and has a degree of artistry.

It also owns the idea of a better budget motel.

"The Ultimate Driving Machine" is simple, brazen and clear. It also owns the idea the kickass driving experience.

The "Away go troubles down the drain" jingle is simple and infinitely catchy, with a degree of artistry to it. (Creating good, insidious jingles is a specialized skill.) This particular jingle also helps Roto-Rooter own the idea of opening drains.

Name any one dominant brand, and they own one dominant idea.

DEATH OF THE ONE, DEATH OF THE BRAND

After college, Blaine worked in a small chain of Boston-based stereo stores that prided themselves in selling equipment that was a cut above.

The company's brand tag line was, "The Land of the Chosen Few."

They focused on a more educated customer with more sophisticated tastes.

There was a competing chain of stereo stores that was much bigger and was often perceived as more of a supermarket, selling equipment that was more mass-market.

The reality?

Other than the size of the respective chains, both chains sold a lot of equipment that was very similar.

But the smaller chain's brand was well-crafted.

By focusing on one thing and one thing only, the company's reputation for quality components and better service propelled it to notoriety as the better, more distinguished choice for a more discriminating consumer.

Because it was The Land of the Chosen Few.

In a way, it was The Ultimate Driving Machine for consumer electronics.

Of course, things change.

Blaine left the stereo sales business and went to sea on big sailing yachts.

And The Land of the Chosen Few was displaced with a new tag line: "For Times Like These."

Really?

What exactly does that mean?

That brand shift, combined with a rapid expansion in an ever-changing marketplace…well, let's just say that lack of potent brand combined with other challenges did exactly what you might expect.

The chain no longer exists.

Neither does the larger competitor it used to be alongside.

And neither does the gigantic supermarket of electronics, Circuit City.

Speaking of which, do you have any idea what Circuit City's brand was? We seem to recall something about it being the electronics retailer where "Service is state of the art."

What does that mean?

That kind of harkens back to The Home Depot's "You can do it, we can help" sentiment. There's a subtext of something just plain wrong.

But getting back to the small electronics chain: there was a distinct shift in what the brand stood for.

"For Times Like These" doesn't really mean anything.

The Land of the Chosen Few had a certain snob appeal. It appears to be about the company's selectivity—but by extension it's about the core customer. It implies that, by shopping there, you too are one of the chosen few.

And if you read the textbook evaluation of what happened to the company, there's a lot of analysis about certain strategic moves and larger economic challenges that led to the demise.

What the textbook case doesn't really address is the abandonment of a brand and with it, the core customer.

They stopped focusing on one thing.

They stopped honoring their one core customer.

They became large and limp and notable for nothing.

They became a "me-too" brand where they had originally been a "this is who we are" brand.

Abandoning your one-thing-and-one-thing-only brand and abandoning your core customer (i.e., a more sophisticated, better-educated individual prepared to spend a little more) and turning yourself into another amorphic big box store is a recipe for disaster.

Think back to Southwest Airlines.

"We are the low cost airline."

Their poetry: "You are now free to move about the country." It's Southwest's lower cost that has given you your freedom. They just found a more memorable way to express it. A way that makes it even more valuable. A way that ironically links to a ubiquitous air travel cliché: the pilot has turned off the seatbelt sign and you are now free to move about the aircraft. It has an amusing, inextricable air travel hook. And let's face it: my freedom is worth even more to me than merely saving a few dollars—which I know I'm gonna do. Southwest really raises the bar for cheap air travel. They transcend even their own pricing. (It also never hurts if you can make good use of the word "free.")

And their stance as "The Low-Cost Airline" hasn't changed at all in the nearly 50 years the airline has been in business.

If Southwest suddenly decided they wanted to compete for the high-end business traveler, and changed all their marketing accordingly, they'd be in deep trouble.

Their one thing is being the low-cost airline in a high-cost airline world.

Their one-thing-and-one-thing-only brand is predicated on delivering that to you. You are now free to move about the country.

But reconciling their low-cost directive with passengers who want to be pampered would never make those pamper-me passengers happy (they're not set up for it and don't know how to do it), and it would create a disconnect with their core customer base.

Southwest wisely remains dedicated to one thing and one thing only.

YOUR ONE THING MUST HONOR YOUR ONE CUSTOMER

Several years back, Honey was working on radio advertising for Hotwire.com. As you probably know, Hotwire is a website where travelers go to find the best deals on hotel rooms, airfare, cruises, etc. Their one thing: offering Hotwire users 4-star rooms at 2-star prices.

Before this ad was ever requested, the advertising agency and client had done their homework. They knew exactly who their client was. They knew their habits and what was important to them. They knew that this was a person who not only looked for the best price online, but took pride in doing the leg work and landing the big prize: the lowest fare or rate.

The folks at Hotwire and their agency also understood this: the best way to talk to their core prospect was by letting him know "we get it." They understood this prospect's behavior, appreciated all the leg work he did in his search for the lowest price, and were in full support of it.

The following was the script that eventually was selected and recorded:

> HOTWIRE RADIO / "Magellan" 60 sec.
>
> ANNOUNCER: You're a hunter. The Magellan of discount internet hotel rates. You'll forage your way through every online travel site for the best price on a fabulous room. And just for you, there's Hotwire.com, where you'll unearth truly thrilling deals on 3 & 4 star hotels.
>
> Like 4 stars in Napa. Travelocity price, $249, Hotwire.com price, just $111. Or 4 stars in Seattle. Priceline retail price, $149. Hotwire.com price, just $94.
>
> You see, my gifted searcher, when hotels have unsold rooms, they use Hotwire to fill them. So you get them at prices lower than any other travel site. Guaranteed. So, go forth and explore all those travel websites for the lowest rates. Then buy

from Hotwire.com, where you'll find 4-star rooms at 2-star prices.

JINGLE: H-O-T-W-I-R-E! Hotwire dot com.

Would this ad have appealed to those people who just want to quickly find a low-ish price and be done with the whole thing?

Probably not.

Did it appeal to the Hotwire audience?

It did in spades. In fact, response to this commercial was so enormous that for the longest time, when she'd be re-introduced in client meetings, Honey was always "the one who wrote 'Magellan.'"

This "Magellan message" spoke directly to Hotwire's core customer in a way that celebrated him. It looked at a personal habit (true enjoyment of the hunt for the best price on a hotel room) and elevated it to legendary proportions.

And while comparing finding a great price on a 4-star hotel room to leading the first expedition to sail from the Atlantic Ocean into the Pacific Ocean may seem a bit over the top, if you yourself have ever scored that great price, you know it's something worth celebrating.

The bottom line is this: people do not have time to pay attention. They do not have the ability to focus on more than one thing at a time.

In an ever-fragmented, split-focused communication environment, being known for one thing and one thing only is more important than ever.

Find your one thing.

Make sure you can be honest and committed about that one thing.

Make sure your one thing honors your core customer.

Take that one thing and live by it.

Then profit from it.

IGNITION POINTS

- The more you try to say with your brand, the more likely your brand will fail.

- People can focus on only one thing at a time, and it is incumbent upon you to show them that one thing—the right thing.
- If you give them too much, they don't know what you stand for.
- One brand concept, conveyed concisely, can be the difference between a prospect feeling nothing and feeling something that matters.
- The Power Of One is part of what has made unglamorous Roto-Rooter a household name for over 50 years.
- Don't confuse the power of the true one thing that matters to your customer with what you think matters to your customer—or what matters to you personally.
- Your one thing must honor your customer.

FIRESTARTER

Think about three strong, national brands and The Power Of their One. What is it? How about locally? Do you know any local businesses—or better yet, direct competitors—who have successfully exercised The Power Of One in their brand?

Chapter 6

BRAND, RINSE, REPEAT

Consistency is so important, it bears repeating.

Consistency is so very, very important, it bears repeating.

Consistency adds up.

Consistency is your friend.

Without consistency, you're inconsistent—which looks a lot like "incontinent," and is, in a way, the same thing.

An inconsistent brand is not a brand.

It's a mess.

Be consistent.

Consistency is very, very important.

Consistency is your friend.

Some might call it redundancy.

We call it money in the bank.

Are we being redundantly clear? If you answered yes, welcome to the world of consistency in branding.

ROME WAS NOT BUILT IN A DAY— AND NEITHER IS YOUR BRAND

You're going to find us banging the drum for a lot of traditional media. Despite the endless reports of their death, we love radio, print, TV and direct mail.

That said, we also appreciate the extraordinary potency of social media, online video, and other non-traditional efforts done properly.

And guaranteed, every single brand established in a non-traditional environment uses a key component of traditional branding: consistency.

It doesn't get as non-traditional as Twitter.

Yet, if you look at everything connected to the Twitter brand, from its look to its communication to its users, every single component is unmistakably part of the brand.

It doesn't come as non-traditional as Facebook. Yet just like Twitter, there's no mistaking any component of the Facebook brand.

Hotwire is certainly a non-traditional brand for our time. Yet traditional media advertising is a central component of its marketing. It's also advertising Honey has helped create for Hotwire's Los Angeles-based advertising agency. And when you see a Hotwire TV commercial, it is unmistakably consistent with the Hotwire brand. It looks like it belongs to Hotwire. And when you go to Hotwire.com, the website is unmistakably, consistently part of the brand. All the pieces look and sound like a part of the whole.

You will never see a Hotwire TV commercial or hear a Hotwire radio commercial or anything else connected to Hotwire that doesn't distinctly remind you of Hotwire.

(SIDEBAR: At this writing, Hotwire has recently evolved their television campaign. To their credit, they did it in a way that keeps the brand fresh without walking away from it. The more things change, the more they stay the same—namely, on-brand.)

So, how does this brand consistency happen?

Not by accident, guaranteed.

In fact, if you look at a brand as non-traditional as Hotwire, and dig deep into the marketing department, you find a philosophy that can be traced back to the heritage of companies as traditional as Proctor & Gamble and the building of traditional, number-one brands in the area of packaged goods.

Anyone who tells you traditional marketing is dead has no idea what they're talking about.

Unfortunately, the consistently repeated message that traditional marketing is dead has been very effective in selling non-traditional marketing.

And the reality is, whether your business is traditional or not, you need traditional consistency to build your brand. You require a traditional commitment to what your brand represents, and a consistent voice across all media, whatever they happen to be.

And it will take time.

Yes, proponents of flash-in-the-pan, get-rich-quick schemes will tell you otherwise. They might even help you generate some quick, short-term profits. But beware: so far, practically all of the efforts we've seen in this arena involve zero brand and 100% transactional thinking, i.e., catering to a price-point or a free-offer mentality rather than appealing to the emotional hook that captures your core customer and leads to better overall, long-term brand health.

Understand, we've done transactional advertising in our time. Blaine has even written a book about it. But it always comes with the caveat that this is not about building brand over the long term. It's about building revenue over the short term.

And here's a warning about exclusively aiming for the short term with offers and giveaways: if you make yourself known for price-break specials to drive traffic, you could easily train your audience to wait for your next price-break deal.

What are you going to do the rest of the year?

We've worked with an excellent consultant for dental offices. She had a client who fell into this very trap. Every October he ran a big, noteworthy teeth whitening special offer.

You can guess what happened: no one ever came to him for teeth whitening at any other time of year.

Truth be told, if we're going to do any transaction-based marketing, like a sale or a giveaway, we prefer to do it under the auspices of a solidly constructed brand.

If your brand is about lofty, high-end widgets, when you have an offer, it will be in a lofty high-end voice. It will come from your solid, established brand. Mr. Folksy, Family-Friendly Widget Store should run a very different sales message. He should run that special with a folksy, family-friendly voice.

The reality of a solidly constructed brand is that it takes time to build.

Sometimes, it takes longer than other times.

BRANDING TO THE CHOIR VS. BRANDING TO THE UNSAVED

A perfect example of how long things can take comes from an advertiser who came to us for re-branding.

We gave his business a new name and a new brand identity.

We advertised him accordingly in the market where his business was already established. For three months, he doubled his new customer base every month. His brand promise resonated quite well in a town where many folks already knew him.

Next, this man opened a new branch in a new town that was significantly different from his original location. Using the same brand promise and the same kind of advertising, it took many more months to establish himself.

There are plenty of other mitigating factors that have nothing to do with our branding work and everything to do with practical considerations at the new location. But the bottom line is: he had to build his brand from the ground up in a place where he had no recognition whatsoever. That takes time.

His progress has been slow and steady, and the results are this: his brand is gradually beginning to resonate with his core customer, who is now finding him—and, of course, loving him.

Because that's the kind of guy he is (loveable), and that's what his branding represents.

The point is, the more you're starting from scratch, the longer you have to keep scratching for people to even begin to feel it. If you can't wait for people to notice, stop right now. It's easy for people who already love you to keep loving you. And in most cases, current customers are your best source of new business. But the proof of your success will be in converting those who don't know you.

The first time Honey did professional stand-up comedy, she had a handful of friends in the room. So, out of comfort, she aimed her first jokes at those people. And of course, they laughed. But did they laugh out of friendly obligation or because the message resonated with them? The only way to know was to turn to the strangers in the room. A scarier proposition for sure. But ultimately rewarding. The strangers were then predisposed to laugh more easily. They were becoming friends.

Your brand needs time to build friends.

It takes time.

But they will come.

CONSISTENCY, MEET HONESTY

In various cases, Blaine has demonstrated a particular affinity for building brands with radio advertising that involve the business owner's voice.

A lot of advertisers would find this a recipe for disaster—and most of the time it is because the commercials feature an advertiser who can't act being given a script that's badly written, and the results are awful.

Blaine's preference is enormously labor-intensive, but the results speak for themselves.

He goes to see the advertiser with recording gear and records the advertiser speaking extemporaneously about the business. Then, those recordings are edited down, cherry-picked for the juiciest sound bites and cut into commercials.

The result is a brand-building effort that is unmistakably unique. The brand is honest and the advertiser can live up to the brand promise—because the advertiser is the one making the promise himself, in his own words and (we hope) from the heart.

In the case of the advertiser mentioned earlier in the chapter, his brand is on the cusp of becoming ubiquitous. When they realize who they're talking to, people will stop the advertiser and practically genuflect.

They feel like they know him.

They love him.

In another case, where the brand building involved an interiors business, the owner was at first mortified by the idea of his non-slick voice in the commercials. But as the brand building effort progressed, the business became more recognizable and—more importantly—much busier.

Why does this work better than a business owner reading from a scripted "Come in today, what are you waiting for" script? Because when Blaine records business owners simply talking, the customer gets to hear the real and true individual. The business owner's genuine, honest self. It resonates and is unique to the advertiser. It also doesn't sound like a bunch of meaningless, "…and our friendly, professional, highly-trained widget staff will handle all your widget needs."

Lack of originality is also lack of honesty. Fight it.

In the case of an appliance superstore in Southern California, Blaine received only one specific marching order: you have to mention the family dog in the advertising.

In most cases, we'd consider this a case of (no pun intended) the tail wagging the dog. Nobody should demand execution over a sound strategy.

However, what was unique about this strategy is that the dog represented something truly different about the store. They were a family business that treated customers like family. And the dog was always in the store—which was why they wanted him mentioned. He was a fixture and customers liked him.

What the advertiser had never understood was that the dog needed to be more than just an afterthought. They merely considered it cute to make a passing reference to the dog.

Blaine refused to do that.

Instead, he made the dog the de facto spokesperson for the business. (He barked near the beginning and end of every commercial and was mentioned a couple of times in the copy.)

The dog became representative of the brand.

Of course, the store owner was mortified when this happened.

Fortunately, he was willing to listen to reason.

The dog stayed.

Additionally, the owner did something that so many advertisers do when a new brand advertising campaign starts: he demanded to know why he wasn't seeing immediate results. He had a new branding campaign, so he should immediately see new customers barking about his branding campaign.

Again, he was willing to listen to reason.

He was patient.

Inside of a year, he changed his tune. When he ran an annual sale—with advertising prominently featuring the dog, of course—he was blown away.

By his approximation, fully half of the customers coming into the store demanded to meet the dog.

In the advertiser's own words: "That dog owns this store."

And in one conversation, when it was pointed out that the only people we were alienating were people who hated dogs, he said, "Fine. I don't want 'em in the store anyway."

The brand was honest, unique, and took close to a year to build. He wasn't afraid that his brand didn't appeal to everyone. Once the brand was established, it became this man's juggernaut.

But a lot of businesses chicken out. They don't have the guts to stick with a brand building effort.

And ultimately, they lose to the businesses with the stomach to commit.

That's not to say a brand-building effort necessarily requires an expensive media budget (though it doesn't hurt). But it does require commitment and patience.

And when honesty rears its head—whether in the form of the sincere voice of a business owner, the bark of the family dog, or a message truly unique in its insight or wording—it hits the audience in a much more meaningful way. Just wait and see. (Key word: wait. Patiently.)

FLASH-IN-THE-PAN IS AS FLASH-IN-THE-PAN DOES

The flipside to consistency is wildly successful, flash-in-the-pan advertising at the expense of good branding.

The typical case is one where an advertiser has no faith in advertising. He wants to "test" it out.

Or, an advertiser is sold a bill of goods by an unscrupulous (or ignorant) advertising salesman.

Either way, here's how it works: the advertiser is convinced he has to make a big offer. It has to be big enough to make people say, "Wow!" and pick up the phone or come into the store immediately.

And it works.

Because people hear or see the message, say, "Wow!" and rush to the phone or rush into the store and buy immediately.

That has nothing to do with branding. This goes back to the old transactional customer bugaboo.

You're not building a relationship between consumers and the brand.

You're building a relationship between consumers and a sale price.

That's not a relationship built on commitment.

It's probably not a relationship you want.

It's a relationship built purely on a transaction.

See also: prostitution.

Are we being harsh?

Perhaps.

But, invariably, even when warned about the pitfalls of running transactional advertising, here's what happens: the advertiser becomes giddy with the idea of fast and easy profits.

Then, when the transactional love affair is over, and the advertiser tries building a brand, nothing happens quickly.

It's not hugely profitable overnight.

And the advertiser freaks out.

He either demands to reinstate the transactional message, or else he stomps away saying this whole branding thing is a lousy idea.

Consistency is a problem.

Commitment is too much work.

He wants less commitment and more transactions.

Which is a problem.

A transaction is a date. (See also: prostitution.)

A brand is a marriage.

And that marriage is between the branded business and the heart and mind of the core customer.

That doesn't mean your business is necessarily marrying the customer (which is always a fabulous thing to have happen). Maybe you're branding the kind of business customers use only once. (See also: burial plots.) Regardless, make your brand top of mind for what that customer will buy only once, and they will come to you. Moreover, they will recommend you—often if they've never even used you. That's how powerful a strong brand is.

There's a good chance you've never needed a drain opening service.

But if your mother's drain was clogged, and she called you to say she was standing ankle-deep in filthy water, might you recommend she call Roto-Rooter?

Maybe not.

But guaranteed, you'd at least think of it.

That's an example of the marriage between you and that brand.

And it's a transactional brand. Most people don't have any kind of a glowing commitment to a drain opening service because they don't need one with any frequency. (You hope.)

But it's a marriage nonetheless. A marriage between you and the idea of what they do. Thanks in large part to a jingle you may not have heard in years.

Ironically, even though it's a transactional brand, transactional advertising probably wouldn't work. You can't really offer a special on "drain opening, today only!"

But if you have a patio furniture store, you can easily have a "20% off sale, this week only!"

And you can get a flurry of customers this week.

They are transactional customers. They're attracted not by any marriage between you and the brand, but by the idea of something great for a low price.

Once the sale is over, so is the flurry of customers.

So, you can start building the brand.

And be mortified at how long it's taking.

You can either bite the bullet and commit—or you can chicken out.

The patio furniture store that Blaine worked with did exactly that: chickened out.

This had happened back when Blaine was a Creative Director at a radio network. An account rep brought the patio furniture store onto the air—and both he and Blaine explained exactly how it should work.

For long-term health, you need to build a brand.

For a quick cash injection, you need a big offer.

The advertiser wanted proof that radio worked, and they opted for the big offer. (See also: prostituting themselves.)

For various reasons related to transactions versus branding, they made some money, they freaked out, and they went away.

Consistency scared them.

Commitment was not in their marketing vocabulary.

Yet they'd been in business for a quarter of a century. Commitment certainly made sense when it came to unlocking the doors every morning.

But commitment didn't extend to building their brand in a time when business was slipping, competition was increasing, and they were losing customers to brands like Home Depot. (Remember them?)

Mr. Patio Furniture didn't trust his audience enough to commit to them. Why should they commit to him?

Now, this isn't to say you can't develop a transactional brand for a retail store. It has been done famously in the guise of New York's infamous electronics chain, Crazy Eddie's.

"His prices are insane!"

Were they really?

Hard to say.

But his reputation was such that people flocked there to buy what they perceived to be deeply discounted prices on electronics.

Of course, many of those customers probably never went back a second time. (Blaine didn't.)

But the reputation was such that if you wanted sizzling gear for discount prices, Crazy Eddie was your man. (Crazy Eddie also went to prison convicted of fraud. But that's another story entirely.)

Also (and this may sound contrary to what we've been preaching), Crazy Eddie's was a solid brand.

Yes, it was based on price alone, but it was a CRAZY price.

There have been many me-too crazy sales guys since then, but Crazy Eddie's was truly notable and iconic.

And commitment? Crazy Eddie's media buy was local, concentrated, and hugely committed.

Despite his limited regional business, his advertising was so notable and his brand was so strong, he became known nationally—unusual for a relatively small, regional operation.

Bottom line: his brand worked for a while.

He wasn't afraid to commit to attract endless flash-in-the-pan customers.

And if your business is going to go the low-price-driven route, you better be ready to live there 100% of the time with a branded sales message.

YOU KNOW THEM BECAUSE THEY ARE RELENTLESS

It may have happened to you.

You're watching TV. A commercial comes on that you've never seen.

And you know almost before you're seven seconds in that this commercial has to be a Target commercial.

Why is that?

Because they are relentless in their consistency.

There is a certain hipness and sense of humor about Target's advertising.

And it's all in keeping with the brand. They are the hipper, funner big box discount retailer.

And truthfully, how much different is Target than Walmart?

Not enormously.

Yes, Target does have a certain degree of hipness in some of its offerings that Walmart doesn't.

But by and large, it's another big box retailer full of discounted commodity merchandise.

Yet their brand makes you feel so much differently about shopping at Target.

You feel like even though you're buying a cheap picture frame, you're hipper than the folks doing the same thing right now at WalMart.

In fact, that brand existed before there was really much difference in what Target sold. Their advertising was very hip and fun—yet when people went to Target, they weren't finding much of that hipness and funness implicitly promised by the brand advertising. There was something of a disconnect.

Eventually, things did change. The Michael Graves designed teapot has probably achieved iconic status for representing the shift in the Target product line.

And Target continues to sell that hip and fun brand with a relentless consistency that should serve as an object lesson for anyone who seems to think they exist in a commoditized marketplace. You can (and must) differentiate your brand.

But you also want to be sure you can deliver on that brand promise.

You have to commit to it.

Of course, you might have a problem with the example of Target because you don't own a multi-billion dollar chain of big box retail stores.

All right then. Maybe Men's Wearhouse is a better example for you. After all, what is there about this huge national brand that isn't achievable for a local business owner? For 18 years, Men's Wearhouse CEO George Zimmer has been appearing in his own advertising, proclaiming "You're going to like the way you look, I guarantee it."

What we have here is a retail clothing store, specializing in men's suits, that targets guys who'd really rather not be shopping for suits.

How do we know this?

Well, you could read the *Bloomberg Businessweek* article from November 2004, in which the reporter talks about this at length: "the neatly displayed clothes in Zimmer's stores [are] designed to cater to the unpretentious guy who wants to do as little as possible to maintain his wardrobe."

In fact, the article opens with a description Zimmer's pre-IPO pitch to potential investors, which included a picture of a man sitting in a dentist's chair. The point was that most men consider shopping for a suit as enjoyable as getting a root canal.

So, really, this is a man who feels quite deeply about his core customer. Who knows exactly who he's talking to and why—and what the better reality is that he wants to offer them.

The *Bloomberg* article also discusses how George Zimmer appears in his own advertisements because he believes he has more credibility than a hired actor. And by all accounts, Zimmer is honestly that guy who you see in those ads: unpretentious, everyman, one of us—to the point where he insists on mixing with his employees. He apparently attends 20 Men's Wearhouse holiday parties across the country every year. Commitment—not just to the brand for his customers, but to the idea of the brand for the people who work for the brand, spreading the gospel of Men's Wearhouse.

George Zimmer portrays himself as a man of the people, he lives up to that portrayal, and his company is every bit what it is designed to be: the suit store for the everyman.

The "You're going to like the way you look, I guarantee it" brand resonates deeply with its core customer—and is relentlessly consistent in making sure it happens that way.

But once again, we're talking about an enormous, publicly traded company with a huge advertising budget.

Nonetheless, the model is entirely scalable. There is no reason on earth why one man with one store can't do one thing consistently the way George Zimmer has.

But what about a huge brand that really doesn't spend much at all on advertising?

Enter Howard Schultz.

You probably know his name.

He's the man who has built a global empire out of a lowly bean.

Howard Schultz is the man behind Starbucks Coffee.

It's a brand with which you are probably familiar.

You know what Starbucks is about: an obsession with high-quality coffee. In the titular words of Howard Shultz's book about the company, it's something he's poured his heart into.

The brand is ubiquitous.

As of this writing, Starbucks has over 17,000 stores in over 50 countries.

When you go to a Starbucks, you know pretty much what to expect. It's a very distinct, very well-defined experience. They spend a lot of time and money trying to create better products and a better customer experience.

In fact, that's their central marketing strategy: making the customer feel the right thing about visiting a Starbucks store.

Relative to other companies their size, Starbucks spends almost nothing on advertising. Yes, there is a reported $40 million marketing budget—and that goes largely to advertising Via instant coffee and packaged Frappuccino. Some years back, before the packaged supermarket products, and before the economy went in the tank, Starbucks' reported advertising budget was just around one-million dollars. For a company of that size, that is a miniscule ad budget.

By and large, Starbucks advertising budget does not go to advertising the brand.

The store itself is the advertisement for the brand.

Because the brand is predicated on serving you with their passion for coffee. In fact, if you read the opening pages of *Tribal Knowledge: Business Wisdom Brewed from the Grounds of Starbucks Corporate Culture*, it says pretty much that. Starbucks never set out to create a brand as much as they set out to give you an experience.

Which, when you boil it right down to its essence, is exactly what we've been saying all along: a brand is how you want people to feel about your business.

And Starbucks has been relentlessly consistent in its delivery of customer experience. They want you to feel something very specific every time you step into one of their stores.

They also execute this brand without any significant advertising budget.

So, you can try to argue that the relentless consistency of Target and Men's Wearhouse don't apply because they're big companies with big ad budgets. (Never mind that they started as small companies.) The big ad budget argument simply doesn't hold water with Starbucks. (They also started as a very small company.)

Certainly, marketing a high-priced luxury item or high-priced professional service is going to differ from selling a high-priced cup of coffee. It's entirely possible that you can't make it work without an advertising budget.

But the point here is not about the amount of ad dollars you have to spend.

It's about how, no matter what you do, you need to be 100% committed to a well-defined brand whose message is unmistakable. A message that knows who it's talking to and what they want and/or need to hear. Smaller brands need consistency most of all. You aren't going to have those huge media dollars and get your message heard 10 times a day. You can't afford to be unfocused.

Consistency makes friends.

Consistency is your friend.

BUT ISN'T CONSISTENCY THE HOBGOBLIN OF SMALL MINDS?

Everybody thinks they know this quote.

And guaranteed, every person who thinks they know it has never read Emerson.

The actual quote is "a *foolish* consistency [emphasis added] is the hobgoblin of small minds."

There is nothing foolish in the consistency of building a brand.

There's a wonderful quote from John Wanamaker, the father of advertising as we know it. Wanamaker owned a famous department store at the turn of the 20th century. And he famously said, "Half of the money I spend on advertising is wasted. The problem is I don't know which half."

In other words, Wanamaker had some idea about the challenges associated with building a brand.

It's a constant effort, and you can never be entirely sure how and where your efforts are paying off because it's a cumulative effect.

This quote can also be used to show the futility of trying to source your leads when you're doing brand advertising, but that's another challenge entirely. For now, we need to consider the engine of your brand.

And speaking of engines, another of our favorite quotes comes from William J. Wrigley, he of the chewing gum. He is reputed to have referred to brand advertising as "the engine that propels our sales." He'd built the Wrigley gum brand through advertising, and he knew he had to continue advertising or be damned to failure. Which is why he kept his advertising running through World War II, even though his product wasn't available to consumers due to lack of top-quality ingredients. Wrigley's limited wartime production was going exclusively to the armed forces. Yet he kept right on advertising the *unavailability of his product.*

When the war ended and product manufacturing resumed, public demand for Wrigley products was higher than ever.

Your brand is the engine. The engine needs to keep running. If you don't commit to fueling it and keeping it tuned, it sputters and dies.

Build it well and keep it running consistently, and it will transport your business quite well.

Long live the engine of brand.

Want another analogy?

OK.

Your brand's job is to make and keep friends. How do you make and keep friends? By being relevant and dependable.

Commit.

Long live your brand's friendships.

IGNITION POINTS

- Relentless consistency is vital to the success of a brand.
- Whether using traditional or non-traditional advertising and marketing, consistency is key.
- It is possible to have quick, flash-in-the-pan successes without consistency—and even without a brand—but it doesn't feed long-term success.
- Building a brand in the minds of the public never happens overnight, but takes time—which is why consistency is so important.
- Consistency in the brand/customer relationship is what builds friendships between the brand and the prospect customer base.
- Relentless consistency is vital to the success of a brand.
- Honesty is a key part of consistency, because you can't fake it for long—people eventually figure it out.
- Being consistently honest is much easier than being consistently fake.
- Flash-in-the-pan, get-rich-quick marketing is incapable of sustaining a brand, as it can't be consistently maintained.
- Get-rich-quick marketing should not be confused with relentlessly consistent discount brand building—which can and does work over the long haul.
- Consistency of brand goes way beyond the advertising and must extend to the typical customer experience every day.
- Relentless consistency is vital to the success of a brand.

FIRESTARTER

Think of three brands that are impactful because of their consistency. Who are they and how are they consistent? Are there any local brands or direct competitors of yours who have opted for this kind of consistency? Are the brands honest and resonant, either for you or for people you know? Do you remember the day you recognized each of these brands? How long did it take for you to become aware of them and what they stand for?

Chapter 7

PUTTING A FIRE IN THE SMALL BUSINESS BRAND

At Slow Burn Marketing, we've faced some interesting challenges with regard to small business branding. What's even more interesting is the reactions that we've received from many of these clients. Some of them have actually cried. (For the right reasons.) Others have been utterly exuberant at the branding efforts executed on their behalf. And we have a theory about all of this.

For the ones who've worked with other marketing professionals, they're experiencing something new. Instead of merely being told, "Here's how you have to advertise to get business," they're being asked questions about why they do what they do. They're being quizzed down to the very core of their being for the reasons why they've chosen their life's work. We're listening to them and delivering a branding package that honestly reflects something they've been trying to capture but which has been elusive for so long. As more than one client has put it, "It's like you totally understand me."

For the ones who've never worked with marketing professionals, the ones who've tried to do it all themselves, they're suddenly not alone. They've been executing marketing and advertising materials for years with no comprehension of the branding process. Suddenly, instead of wearing a T-shirt with a saying on it, their business has a full suit of custom tailored clothing that fits and makes sense.

In either case, we figure it this way: it's almost like therapy.

They get to talk.

We get to listen.

They get results.

That probably sounds a lot simpler than it really is, but the bottom line is: rebranding a small business is about getting to the juicy core of what you do and why.

Honey helped do that for over two decades working with some of the biggest brands in the nation.

Blaine helped do it for almost two decades working with some of the smallest, most potent brands in local business.

As Slow Burn Marketing, we've done it for various, carefully chosen clients who all have one thing in common: they're not afraid to work hard, and they're not afraid of commitment to a brand identity.

Here now, just a few examples of small business brands that we've enjoyed creating for people who love doing what they do.

BRAND AND THE EYE DOCTOR

United Eye Care Specialists. It sounds like the name of a big, monolithic company that might work with insurance companies or provide products to opticians or just about anything except what it was: a small eye doctor's office in a little professional strip by a regional hospital in rural New Hampshire.

We're talking one hard-working optometrist named Dr. Samuel Giveen, and his staff of three. At the time, they were the sum total of United Eye Care Specialists.

Let's also be clear about something: this is a man who bought the business. He did not name it. The name came with the package.

Let's also be clear about something else: this man is an excellent eye doctor.

He graduated from the nation's most prestigious optometry school. He teaches other eye doctors. He is a volunteer optometrist for the InfantSEE program, which offers free eye exams to kids under one year old. He's been recognized by the American Optometric Association for his work.

This man is an optometrist's optometrist.

He's also a very personable, friendly guy. He's no-nonsense, very New England, and has the utmost integrity.

That's why, in our estimation, the United Eye Care Specialists brand was so unfortunate for him. It sounded as impersonal as he is personable.

For Honey, the name had evoked the aroma of an institutional hospital hallway. Cold. Antiseptic. No heart.

So, we say unto you, if you don't think that the name of your business matters, if you don't think it makes folks form an immediate opinion, take a deep whiff and think again.

United Eye Care Specialists also had no consistency of image. Print ads didn't look anything like the collateral material, and various versions of the logo didn't match each other on either the signage or the advertising.

There was no consistency of image, other than each image evoking only a cold and unengaged corporate entity.

We spent a long time talking with the doctor as well as with his operations manager (who also happens to be his new wife and previously a long-time regional manager with Starbucks—so she was entirely understanding of the notion that a brand should make people feel something).

After many discussions and after a couple of weeks of hashing it out between Honey and Blaine, we finally hit on three possible brands for the good doctor.

The one that he ultimately chose made plenty of sense as far as we were concerned: he ditched United Eye Care Specialists for Dr. Sam's Eye Care.

Why did he like this for his new name?

Well, as one of his subsequent direct mail ads said to its recipients, "You can't shake Dr. United's hand."

The core customer for the Dr. Sam's Eye Care brand is about as simply defined as it gets: Mom. Here's what the brand exploratory had to say about our core customer and the brand:

> While there's a lot of talk about Primary Care Providers in the context of medical dialogue these days, there is essentially only one primary care provider worth discussing: Mom.
>
> Mom observes and makes medical decisions for herself, her children, often for her husband, frequently for her parents, and possibly even for her in-laws. Mom is the constant. Whether stated explicitly or made more implicit, each message must appeal to Mom's sensibilities. The secondary target is anyone who appreciates the kind of care associated with Mom.
>
> The brand must evoke compassion, competence and caring. From giving the simplest eye exam to meeting profound vision challenges, we must become top of mind for anyone considering vision care. People should like the doctor's brand well before they ever need the doctor.

Every print advertisement that emanates from Dr. Sam's Eye Care, every radio commercial, every tweet, every Facebook post, everything on the website—all of it is informed by the fact that we're speaking to a New Hampshire mom—and by the fact that Dr. Sam is a straight ahead, no-nonsense guy. As it happens, Dr. Sam's no-nonsense demeanor also informs the tag line that appears in every one of his advertisements: "Straight Talk. Better Vision."

Additionally, we created a new logo for Dr. Sam's Eye Care. The original logo was a somewhat sterile typeface accompanying a hard and rigid iris design that the good doctor had commissioned himself. He was proud of that iris, and it symbolized many things to him. While not under direct orders to keep the iris, it was obviously preferred that we do so.

Ultimately, the resulting logo was a softer, more welcoming sans-serif font that says "Dr. Sam's Eye Care," stacked over a version of the iris that was softened through the use of color.

From this brand position, all of Dr. Sam's business materials were created using the new logo and tag line. All his business cards, his stationary, his collateral, his website (which he'd never had until now), everything looked—and more importantly, *felt*—as if it came from the same place.

Think back to Target and their red and white bullseye. It's on every TV spot, print ad, postcard, billboard, and web page. Over and over again. It's there to train the audience to know who's talking to them before anyone ever starts talking…or singing. It's no different for a small business.

We created an advertising campaign of radio, direct mail and print advertising informed by the Dr. Sam's "Straight talk, better vision" brand. The advertising spoke directly to people, in plain English, the way that Dr. Sam would speak to them—so much so that the printed headlines are always in quotes and attributed to Dr. Samuel Giveen.

"We work Sundays because you don't."

"Eye doctors shouldn't have fine print."

"Ever wonder what happens at an eye-care open house? Me too."

"Our screws don't fall out."

Here's the copy from one of the radio commercials—which was created not from a script, but from extemporaneous recordings of conversations with Dr. Sam. The announcer is not a smiling, oblivious voice with unengaged stentorian demeanor, but a low-key human whose tone contrasts appropriately with Dr. Sam's own soft-spoken style. The music underneath them is a happy, strolling, old-timey jazz piece with clarinet and piano.

> DR. SAM: Ya know, we call ourselves primary healthcare practitioners, but I think we're always really secondary. Mom's primary.

ANNCR: When it comes to the littlest patients at Dr. Sam's Eye Care, Dr. Sam sees who really calls the shots. And when those little patients get their glasses…

DR. SAM: It's thrilling. They put on their glasses…I've had kids, ya know, the classic is, "Wow I never knew that there were leaves on the trees and that's how they got on the ground." (LAUGHS) I had a kid one time who came back just after having had a pair of glasses fitted. He didn't know what telephone poles were. Didn't know why they were there. He'd never seen the wires before. That's pretty exciting.

ANNCR: And, as exciting as it is, Dr. Sam knows who's ultimately responsible for those kids getting those glasses.

DR. SAM: When it comes to kids, mom makes the health care decisions. Mom wasn't educated in this. But she often knows what to do.

ANNCR: For common sense care and uncommonly sensible rates, Dr. Sam's Eye Care…in Claremont on Dunning Street by Valley Regional Hospital. Call 543-20-20. 543-20-20. Dr. Sam's Eye Care. Straight Talk. Better Vision.

Any hard sell happening here? Does it seem like a typical small-market radio commercial? Does anyone talk about "serving all of your eye care needs, convenient location, well-trained staff, or that you should "wait—there's more?"

No way.

What it does is convey the Dr. Sam's brand in a human, approachable way calculated to make you feel something—the *right* thing—about Dr. Sam.

Interestingly, some of the local competition have heard these commercials and have responded by trying to buff and polish their own marketing accordingly.

And while their efforts are sincere, even appropriately human in some cases, they still lack what Dr. Sam has: a unique, distinct and consistent brand focus.

Also, for anyone who claims traditional advertising is dead, know this: during the first three months of the campaign, which was comprised primarily of local radio and newspaper advertising, the Dr. Sam brand doubled his new patient base.

Moreover, his business had been essentially flat for three years. Over the first 10 months of advertising the Dr. Sam's Eye Care brand, business went up 35%.

BRANDING YOUR GOOD HAIR DAY

Do a Google search, in quotes, on the name "ooh la la hair salon." As of this writing, it yields almost 42,000 results, representing hair salons from Morrisville, Vermont to San Francisco, California.

One of those salons happens to be in Park City, Utah.

It happens to be where Honey and Blaine get their hair cut.

And no, neither Honey nor Blaine is the kind of person who would seek out a salon named Ooh La La.

We are the kind of people who would listen to one of the most valuable forms of advertising: word of mouth.

And the word of mouth was coming in very positive for Ooh La La.

It's a surprisingly busy salon upstairs in a commercial strip near downtown Park City. There's a good energy, and it's just hip enough to make you think maybe you're in the right place without being so hip that you feel like you're wearing a Brooks Brothers Suit in the mosh pit.

The problem at Ooh La La was the brand.

The name and logo came along with the business when the owner bought the salon from its founder.

The current owner is a tall woman, willowy, short hipster haircut, bleached blond, tattoos, and a cheery demeanor. She's a girl who grew up in a Utah cow town, and is the kind of entertaining urban-meets-rural contradiction that seems to be uniquely a product of the 21st century.

Why is this important?

The personality of the owner is always important. It almost always drips down into the business and affects how people feel about it.

If a business owner is fastidious, patrons will know. If he's funny and lighthearted, people will know. If he's a slob, people will know.

The owner's personality should inform a brand's tone and keeps the marketing honest.

Of course, the target customer also factors into the brand equation, but still: you must be quite clear on who you are as a business owner. (Check with your therapist if necessary.)

So, she has a salon in possibly one of the hippest small towns in the American west. Park City was a fairly low-key ski resort town until a combination of the Winter Olympics and the Sundance Film Festival changed things.

We have friends who, as hippies back in the '70s, talked of walking into the "wrong bar" in Park City. We know people who, in the '80s, were ski bums who lived in apartments along Main Street. Today, amongst the film stars and fashionistas whose Porsches and G-Wagens fill the streets, where repeated calls for "affordable work force housing" seem like whistling into the wind, the wrong bars and ski bum apartments are but a fond memory. Today, Park City has an element of high-end hipster central.

Ooh La La's owner knew that Ooh La La had an element of… something else.

The name is kind of a cliché.

And while the original logo probably looked fine when it was created, it was now looking a little cheap and outdated. A cursive, all lower-case font, magenta on white, Honey has commented that it looked like something a school girl might have doodled on her notebook cover.

In a town that is becoming ever-more sophisticated, Ooh La La's brand appearance was stuck in an earlier, less sophisticated time.

The first thing we did was look at what was right about the brand: the owner and her attitude. Her demeanor and good nature inform everything about the business. Her youth, her energy, her creative sensibilities—she represents everything the logo did not. And while she isn't glossy, there's something enjoyably earthy and honest about her and her place.

Then, there was the brand name. While it might not have been the most desirable reflection of the management's demeanor, it was a known name in a business where that can be everything. The owner was reluctant to part with it. Changing the name wasn't really an option.

So, keeping the name, we evolved the Ooh La La look.

Taking a cue from the owner and who she is, the look became more youthful and more hip, with a bit of an edge. The cursive "Ooh La La" was refined to look more sophisticated. Then, it was placed inside of a banner. The banner was draped across a stylized, cut-paper-look winged heart. The wings have an edgy, almost metallic motif. The logo looks almost as if it could have come off a hip Hollywood bar or tattoo parlor. Ooh La La's new tag line: "Love. Truth. Hair."

It's fun. It's young. It's potentially aspirational for those who are neither hip nor young. It looks more current without alienating. It has a sense of humor about itself.

It is a much more accurate representation of the woman who runs the show.

Ooh La La changed the signs, business cards (important, since they double as appointment cards), gift certificates and brochure, and built a website. It all matched. It was all a cohesive effort.

Then came the advertising.

Previous advertisements very much had that look of, "Well, how do we make this look like an advertisement?" combined with "how do we make people understand this is a massage parlor?"

In other words, the ads had some challenges.

We've shown old Ooh La La ads at live events, and people have said they thought it was an advertisement for an escort service.

The name Ooh La La, the purple zebra-striped border around the ad, the cute girls posing in the ad—none of it really conveyed quite the right message. Unless the message was, "Now featuring ex-Hooters girls."

The new advertisements feature the logo as the main image with the "Love, Truth, Hair" tag line. The headlines say things like, "Feed Your Head," "Wax On, Wax Off," and "Deny Your Roots." All as irreverent as the logo. And all credit goes to the owner for being brave enough to move forward with ads that aren't your standard "proudly cutting Park City's hair for over XX years."

People enjoy the new look and enjoy the ads.

And we know they're working.

Whenever they run in the local paper, the phone rings and the website experiences a huge spike in traffic. (As is typical in many small businesses, the salon manager wasn't informed that the ads had started running and couldn't figure out why call volume was suddenly way up. If you're running new advertising, tell your staff. They need to know.)

It's a fun brand that people are happy to embrace. It's a club that's fun to join, if only for your monthly hair cut.

And, the primary advertising medium at the moment is local newspaper supported by a website. Traditional media is not dead. But it is much easier to be seen and recognized if your brand says something that matters to people—even it's for something as relatively superficial as a haircut. (And, increased revenue is never superficial.)

BRANDING THE GLOBE

A fellow wanted to hire us to create the brand for his business. He's probably one of the people who helped us create the joke that we specialize in turning down new business.

We turned him down three times.

Yet he kept coming back.

The fourth time he approached us, his vision was finally clear and refined enough that we agreed to take him on.

This was not a re-branding effort. This was building the brand from the ground up. The only existing component was a URL: www.planetdo.com.

Among our tasks: define PlanetDo in one, succinct thought. An elevator pitch, if you will.

It took quite a while.

The one that finally made us happy was surprisingly not clever or fancy. What it was, was clear: PlanetDo is the world's first social network and comparison shopping site dedicated to the active outdoor market.

How much fun is it to be the world's first anything?

And fun is the operative word here.

PlanetDo absolutely has to be fun.

Maybe we need to backtrack just a little here. For anyone who doesn't know what the active outdoor market is, know this: if it's a human- or gravity-powered sport, it probably has a place on PlanetDo.

That means skiers, snowboarders, cyclists, backpackers, hikers, runners, swimmers, climbers—anyone who participates in a sport that can be outfitted at REI is a potential user of PlanetDo. The site includes social networking, comparison shopping, trail maps, event listings, its own video channel, reviews, original content, connections to outfitters, retailers, resorts, etc., and tips and tricks on how to best enjoy it all.

What's interesting about PlanetDo is the core customer. Imagine a 20-something who spends all his time outdoors, doing the sports he loves to do. He has plenty of free time and plenty of money to go skiing, snowboarding, mountain biking, rock climbing, camping—in short, you might consider him a hipster ne'er do well.

Sounds like a pretty small market, doesn't it?

And therein is the beauty of PlanetDo. In some ways, it takes its cues from a toy maker for which Honey used to help create advertising: Nerf.

This might sound crazy, but Nerf products are aspirational.

For instance, many of their products are marketed at 13 year old boys.

Even though the kids who buy those products are 10.

How does that make sense?

There's nothing a 10-year-old boy wants quite as much as to be a 13-year old boy.

Hence, Nerf is aspirational.

The PlanetDo demographic is ultimately anyone who'd rather be out there doing stuff instead of sitting behind a desk, making the money required to take a couple of weeks' vacation at their favorite ski resort.

In fact, if you look at the entire active outdoor market, it's arguable that everything is marketed like Nerf products. Go into an REI store, and you can find all kinds of gear that's good enough to get you to the top of Everest.

Does anyone really need gear that good for a long weekend camping trip to the Sierras? Heck no.

But they buy it anyway.

Many brands of skis are marketed to a 20-something sensibility.

And if you look at the huge cross section of people who are on the slopes, riding those skis, they're a lot older than 20.

The North Face is a hugely popular line of active outdoor clothing. If you look at photos of hardcore mountaineers, you're almost guaranteed to see their logo.

It's also guaranteed you'll see their logo on a lot of folks walking around Manhattan, where the most challenging summit is at the end of an elevator ride.

This doesn't mean that PlanetDo isn't interested in the 20-something hipster who has nothing but free time and money to burn. On the contrary, the more 20-something hipsters the brand attracts, the better.

But the bigger picture of the brand is this: in its effort to be a kind of grown-up Nerf, PlanetDo needs to do certain things. It needs to be somewhat edgy—but not too edgy. It still needs to be accessible. It needs to be fun—but not too "inside" in its fun. It needs to be relevant without being too arcane. It needs to have a clubby element to it without being exclusionary.

In short, it needs to let people in on the good time.

Why does all of this matter? Why does an active outdoor social network and comparison shopping site need to have such a carefully defined, cohesive brand?

Because the three-word phrase "active outdoor market" represents many billions of dollars in products and services worldwide.

And if PlanetDo can attract only a tiny fraction of the advertising dollars used to market those products and services, it's going to make our client very wealthy.

And the only way to attract those dollars is by attracting the right audience.

And the only way to attract the right audience is by having a well-defined brand identity that people recognize.

The best way to attract the right people is to make them feel the right thing.

And making them feel the right thing starts with the logo and the tag line.

The PlanetDo logo has an attitude. It's a vaguely punk, broken font which, instead of an "O" in "Do," has a hand-drawn globe with a stylized, cut-paper feel. It's edgy without being too edgy. It's hip without taking itself too seriously. It also has a contained energy to it, and it looks almost as if it's in motion. Which is good. Because the tagline says: "Uniting a World That Can't Sit Still."

Think about this for a moment. Uniting a World That Can't Sit Still. None of these words is unusual. No one will call you a pseudo-intellectual for saying them. Yet, they stand out. It's because these words had never been linked together in quite this way. It's almost poetic in its expression of the thought. We've discussed the importance of poetry. Also, it's a call to action. A bit of a rallying cry. It's positive and it pulls. Not being able to sit still, a quality people are often put down for, becomes a good thing. An enviable quality. You're one of those special people who gets out and does. Unite. Join. You are special.

PlanetDo is about people who want to get out and Do.

In the parlance of PlanetDo, users are referred to as Doers.

There are tiers of Doers, from Casual Doers to Uber Doers.

PlanetDo has a mobile mascot, if you will: a six-wheeled Swiss Army surplus vehicle called a Pinzgauer. Heavily customized for PlanetDo, this "DoGauer" has a giant logo on the side and a roof rack which makes an excellent platform for throwing T-shirts to Doers at live events. It has tons of personality and strikes an amusing balance between imposing and ridiculous. The DoGauer even has its own feed online at the PlanetDo.com "DoStream."

Since social media is at the core of PlanetDo's business model, we created a video production arm for PlanetDo called DoVision. The DoVision crew goes out and covers crazy events like end-of-ski-season pond skimming competition and skiing Santa Clauses at Christmas. They cover mundane events like active outdoor trade shows and bring a little bit of craziness to the presentation. And these little videos are starting to be embraced by international vendors who are even using them on their own sites as product demos. DoVision also creates its own niche series like *Scar Stories.* People sit in front of the DoGauer and talk to the camera, telling their crazy stories of fun times gone wrong with head-over-heels yard sales that end in blood-stained trips to the ER or the nearest bar. Everyone has a Scar Story—even Nordic Combined Olympic gold medalist Billy DeMong, who sat down for our cameras and told some great stories about going off a ski jump face-first.

One phrase popular in the vernacular of certain active outdoor doers is "hucking your meat." It means throwing yourself off some kind of cliff or other edifice into the air for the thrill of it. Accordingly there's a PlanetDo T-shirt that says, "It's a hucking off point." One woman gave back the free T-shirt because (despite all assurances to the contrary) she thought it was dirty and refused to give it to her teenage son. The PlanetDo CEO was wearing the shirt in a McDonald's (the happy place to buy a hamburger) when an elderly man approached him and said, "You should be arrested!" He refused to believe it wasn't dirty.

The PlanetDo brand is not for everyone.

And PlanetDo is OK with that.

Because the people who do get it? They embrace it that much more completely. They are inside the club. It makes them special.

Those are the people who, no matter what age they are, are going to enjoy talking about their latest conquest on the slope, their favorite scar stories, and who they annoyed with their "hucking off point" T-shirt.

PlanetDo is uniting a world that can't sit still.

HOW MUCH BETTER DO YOU FEEL NOW?

The Greek deity Chronos is said to be the pre-Socratic personification of time. Apollo represents many, many different things—including medicine and health.

So, you probably now know exactly what happens at a business named Chronos Apollo. Right?

No?

Hmm.

Therein lay the challenge with Chronos Apollo, an "Anti-Aging, Wellness and Medical Aesthetics Clinic" that came to us for re-branding.

We have to admit, there is something kind of cool about the name. Chronos Apollo has a certain ring to it.

It also leaves virtually everyone mystified about what they do.

That typically included the well-to-do, successful, middle-aged woman at the core of their target market.

What we were confronted with was a delightful woman who, as an MD, is utterly committed to making people feel and look better. The patient who comes to her is typically feeling endlessly tired, possibly looks beaten down, and is often suffering from a general malaise that in no way leads to any kind of quality of life.

Without going into great detail about her depiction of the medical system in her country, let it suffice to say that it sounds like things have simply been over-institutionalized to a point where there is very little true care. People can't talk to doctors. Doctors don't have time to listen. Patients come through on a conveyor belt and treatments are dispensed. And only one medical problem at a time may be discussed. There are no appointments where a patient can say, "Oh, there's this other problem I'm having with my…" Stop. Make another appointment.

This doctor we were working with has nothing but time for her patients.

They talk.

She listens.

Based on each patient's unique circumstances, she devises a course of treatment to help her patients feel more vital, more youthful, more alive.

Some of the treatments might be traditional. Others might be homeopathic or naturopathic. Acupuncture might be involved. Laser skin treatments could be part of the regimen. It all depends on the patient's unique circumstances.

And does this all work?

Read the letters from her patients.

They rave.

Women who had been suffering under a gray cloud, living dreary and sometimes even chronically painful lives describe extraordinary relief and joyous renewal.

Where a typical doctor might just listen to the problem, write a prescription and move on to the next patient, the Chronos Apollo experience was very different.

As a patient, you had no choice but to participate in the treatment.

And the result is utter transformation.

It is really, really difficult not to like this doctor and her entire modus operandi.

And on the face of it, the branding solution seems almost painfully simple.

The name of her clinic is now…

Better.

The tag line is "Feel. Look. Live."

The attitude is upscale. Think: private club. The logo is elegant and distinguished with an air of Tiffany about it. This is an elective course of treatment often undertaken by wealthy women or female business executives. These are women who believe they deserve better—often the best. Accordingly, the brand's upscale appearance and vaguely Tiffany-esque evocations are no accident.

Chronos Apollo may have possibly left the core customer inferring the right thing—but not likely.

With Better, there is no doubt.

Now described as "A Medical Center for Complete Living," the Better brand is all about the emotional charge associated with being a patient there. And the word medical was very important. This is a doctor, not an aromatherapist. Not to knock aromatherapy, but we need to be clear that there is a medical degree involved here.

Chronos Apollo, while certainly having a nice, clever, intellectual appeal to it, doesn't really let anyone know what it is or does. It could be an upscale gym for men. (After all, Chronos and Apollo were both male deities.)

It could be a fine jewelry store specializing in fiery timepieces. (Remember, Apollo drove that chariot around the earth, hauling the sun each day.)

Chronos Apollo could even be a fancy Greek restaurant.

Better is about feeling, looking and living…well, better.

It also allows for a certain amount of exclusive fun.

A lot of the patients who go to this doctor don't want to tell anyone.

Of course, when they emerge from their treatments rejuvenated and joyful, their friends are bound to ask.

"What have you done?"

"I got better."

The name doesn't get aggressive with absolutes. When presenting the name, we were asked, "Well, what about Best? Don't I want to be the Best?"

Nope.

Because that becomes a grand assertion and can even be an affront. You say you're Best? You're now forced to prove it.

But Better?

There's an inarguable quality to degrees of improvement. You don't have to prove any ultimate. You merely have to promise a degree of positive change.

And if someone says they are already at their best, well, guess what: you're even better.

And what's truly fun about this brand is the client's embrace.

She has totally committed to it.

Chronos Apollo offered a certain intellectual satisfaction.

And as we all know, nobody buys intellectually.

But Better has offered her an emotional charge that is easy to rally behind, get fired up about, and bring to her staff, her patients, to everything about her marketing.

Dr. Sam's Eye Care, with its "Straight Talk, Better Vision" ethos, totally fits the man behind the brand. He is a no-nonsense, commonsense, straight-ahead New England doctor who wants you to avoid glaucoma by eating your leafy greens.

Better, with its "Feel, Look, Live" dynamic, is much different.

It's a totally elective medical service, targeted specifically at women with money, presented by a woman who herself is elegant, bubbly, excited—in fact, she is everything that her patient wants to be.

Want to feel, look and live better?

You're in the right place.

BRANDING FOR THE C-WORD

It's a word nobody wants to hear: "Cancer." Unfortunately, when you hear it in reference to your own diagnosis, you are required to move—despite the potential paralysis of fear. But if you happen to be in Florida, we know one doctor who has an extraordinary bedside manner and is an excellent resource for those afflicted.

And when he came to us, the name of his clinics did not reflect either the quality of his care or his demeanor.

For example, one of his clinics was called Coastal Cyberknife. If you're familiar with cancer treatment, you may have heard of the Cyberknife. It's an advanced form of radiosurgery that is controlled via an enormous robotic arm. It's apparently a boon in cancer treatment.

It also isn't necessarily the first name you want to hear or the first machine you want to see when you've been diagnosed with cancer. When you're reeling from such a diagnosis, you need a friend.

Yet when you logged onto the web page for Coastal Cyberknife, you saw that giant, *Star-Trek*-looking mechanical arm focused on a man lying on his back that we talked about earlier. The patient looks very small and insignificant—and very much like a victim—in this photographic equation.

Coastal Cyberknife was just one of this doctor's three clinics. They all operated under different names. Our job, as we saw it, was to create a brand that could be used as an umbrella for all three, bringing them all together under the same brand.

Here's the thing that we found so extraordinary about these clinics: the doctor himself.

As a child in India, his world was shaken when two important people in his life were diagnosed with cancer. A career in oncology became his life's mission. And the more we spoke to this man, the more we became convinced he was one in a million.

This man is intent on a dialogue with each of his patients. He doesn't just issue a course of treatment as an authority as so many doctors do. This is a man who takes a personal interest.

This is a doctor who gives patients his personal cell phone number. He tells them to call if they have any questions, any time.

For people who can feel very alone in a diagnosis, this is a doctor who works to make them know he's there for them. Think about that: a cancer surgeon who's not only willing to listen, but to then say, "Here's my personal phone number. Feel free to use it." And yes, he makes house calls.

The re-branding discussion took various twists and turns. And ultimately, the brand that won out is the brand that not only fits him best—but best represents what he means to the people he serves.

> One to One Cancer Treatment Center.
>
> Tag line: "It's personal."
>
> The position for One to One is best summarized by what the brand's new manifesto says:
>
> Cancer is a frightening diagnosis. The person coming to One to One is often scared, confused and feeling out of control. Unlike many cancer centers, we don't identify the patient by her illness. We recognize the patient as an individual who is the sum of her experiences. We want to talk to her and listen to her. We may be the first cancer treatment professionals who've done that. In the One to One equation, patient and doctor are equally important. It's about listening, then making an informed decision...together

If you've ever known anyone who had a cancer diagnosis and subsequently felt railroaded by a "doctor of authority," you understand how significant this position is. Granted, some people want that authoritative and detached treatment. If that works for them, excellent. But they aren't going to get that kind of treatment at One to One, so there's no reason to even pretend that One to One is right for that patient.

Equally important in the One to One brand is the mission—again, quoted here from the brand manifesto:

> To treat people as people. Then, they can begin their journey with us in a more optimistic and confident state of mind. If any of our loved ones received a cancer diagnosis, this is how we'd want them to be treated. So everyone who comes to a One to One Cancer Treatment Center is, in essence, a loved one.

One of the most significant words here, for us, is "love." Businesses that truly love their customers have a leg up on the competition. That love permeates everything about their brand and their customer experience. In Hollywood, where the idea of star quality is enormously important, they say that a star has a quality that "prints." That means a star has an essence that is captured on film unlike anything else. In a brand, that love for the customer also prints. It becomes an integral, almost tangible quality in everything about the business.

At One to One, we've made that love for the patient a part of the brand because it does indeed print. When you talk to the good doctor, it's undeniable.

Now, this doesn't mean we're expecting One to One to come right out and say "we love our patients" in their marketing. To explicitly say as much weakens the brand. Generally speaking, if you have to proclaim such a quality, it brings the quality into question. Actions speak louder than words. By showing the love, making people "feel" the love, by behaving in a way that demonstrates a genuine love for their patients, they support the brand and make a much stronger case for their uniqueness.

In the final analysis, this is still a medical treatment.

There's a chance that the patient-centric demeanor of One to One might not be for everyone.

But that's OK. There are still plenty of cancer treatment clinics out there for people who would much rather work with a professional who behaves with detached, clinical authority.

But if you want a partner in your treatment, if you want a doctor who sympathizes and is always there for you, One to One is on your side. Why? Because It's Personal. The Cyberknife? Not so much…

THE MOST IMPORTANT PERSON IN ALL OF THESE BRAND EQUATIONS?

You.

The prospect.

Granted, you personally may not be in the market for a Park City haircut or a central Florida cancer treatment.

But others are.

And each of those "others" who are in the target demographic figures prominently in each of these brands.

The brand is about the person seeking out the product or service.

Equally as important, the brand is about the business owner—but not as in, "Look at me!" Many business owners are very pleased with themselves and think it really is all about them and their acumen. Once upon a time, Blaine had been assigned to work with a chiropractor in an effort to create new advertising. He sat there with the doctor in an effort to find out what was so great about the chiropractor and what he offered his patients. The doctor could never tell him. All he could do was talk about himself. All roads about the patient led back to the chiropractor. That's not useful, nor is it possible to build anything constructive from that.

These brands are about the business owners in the regard that they are there to serve. These proprietors know that the most important person in the brand equation is the customer. Their brands are about themselves only inasmuch as they represent their mission of servitude.

Granted, we're talking about a spectrum here.

The mission at Ooh La La Hair Studio is of different gravity than the mission at One to One Cancer Treatment Center. Good hair is not typically a life or death matter. Plenty of people would be happy to trade their positive cancer diagnosis for a bad hair day.

Nonetheless, all these brands have that mission of servitude in common. They are honest representations of the people who serve, designed to resonate with the customers they serve.

Honest. Resonant. Focused.

And customer-centric.

Key components in the creation of any small business brand.

IGNITION POINTS

- Defining a small business brand requires understanding why you do what you do down to the very core.
- Defining a small business brand requires deeply knowing and understanding the core customer.
- Defining a small business brand requires standing apart from a crowd of me-too competitors, whether in the local neighborhood or in the vast online environment.
- You can't just slap together pointless things because "they kinda look and sound like a brand."
- The difference between United Eye Care Specialists and Dr. Sam's Eye Care is the difference between looking like a giant, faceless corporation that doesn't know or care about anyone, and a personable country doctor who is deeply concerned about what Mom feels.
- The difference between Ooh La La, the salon adrift, and Ooh La La the fun, hip salon that's about "Love, Truth, Hair," is the difference between a salon with no identity, and a salon that knows who it is, why it is the way it is, and why you should come on in and trust them with your hair.
- The difference between Chronos Apollo, the wellness clinic, and Better, A Medical Center for Complete Living, is the difference

between uncertainty and possible pseudo-science, and the reassurance of sound medical treatments.

- The difference between Coastal Cyberknife and One to One Cancer Treatment Center is the difference between focusing on the equipment—and focusing on the patient.
- The most important person to consider in any branding effort is the customer—that's who the brand is ultimately all about.

FIRESTARTER

Think of three brands where you have no doubt the company is all about you. Then, if it's even possible to remember them, think of three brands that seem to be all about the seller. (Don't worry if you can't—being forgettable is what these brands do best.) How does a good, customer-focused brand make you feel about doing business with them, versus doing business with a brand where there is no customer focus—or worse, when the brand feels anti-customer?

Chapter 8

BRAND: HARD WORK, FEAR & LOATHING

So, what is your brand? How do you go about finding that one honest, resonant, customer- centric brand that puts you head and shoulders above your competitors?

We won't kid you: it's work.

Hard work.

We've said this before: don't let the seemingly effortless appearance of some of these brands fool you. They did not fall fully-formed from our heads as if they were Athena springing fully-formed from the head of Zeus.

That said, there is one part of that whole Athena-from-Zeus's-head story that people don't typically take into account: before Athena was born, Zeus was complaining of terrific headaches.

He demanded that his head be split open with blacksmithing tools.

Presumably, that means things like hammers, chisels and anvils.

In a flurry of pre-Athenian brain surgery, Zeus' head was split wide with great and likely painful effort, and Athena was brought unto the Olympian world.

So, maybe it could be said that the brands do indeed fall fully-formed from our heads—after we endured extended headaches and a workout with heavy metal implements.

If your brand ever does materialize spontaneously, fine. It does occasionally happen. Embrace it freely.

Otherwise, prepare to knuckle down and do some work.

Especially since the most difficult brand to create is your own.

And whether you're doing it yourself or working with a professional, here's one of the biggest challenges you're going to face when it comes to building your business's brand: yourself.

BEWARE THE MUSICAL TRAGEDY TWINS

We talk about this in all of our materials related to branding and advertising: beware Fear & Ego. They are your enemies. They will lead you down the circuitous and merry road to marketing hell.

Why do we repeat this with such frequency?

Because we are all human. We all have fears and we all have ego. They are useful at times. The trick here is training them to take a nap.

Fear & Ego have undermined so much good marketing. It's impossible to stress just how serious this is.

For instance, we've talked about how important it is to stand for one thing and one thing only.

Ego says, "Yes, I know, but I'm different than everyone else. I'm special. My mother told me so. I don't need to stand for just one thing. I can stand for all of these things here. It will work for me… the special one!"

Guess what?

Ego is wrong.

You are no different than anyone else attempting to brand a business.

You MUST stand for one thing and one thing only.

Standing for one thing and one thing only is how you win.

Standing for seven things is, in essence standing for nothing.

Fear says, "We can't possibly make do with just one thing! Otherwise, nobody will know we have these other six things! We have to stand for seven things or we won't be able to compete. Mommy!"

Fear is wrong (and a big baby).

Marketing decisions made from a position of fear are always bad decisions.

Honey's father, a longtime entrepreneur and horse-racing handicapper, likes to say that "scared money never wins." It's now officially in print. Honey's father is right.

Successful branding requires having the courage and the wisdom to defeat Fear & Ego—or, as we like to refer to them in an effort to undermine their obvious power, Fred & Ethel.

You remember Fred & Ethel.

They were the nutty neighbors on the *I Love Lucy Show*.

They practically always were there to help fuel some kind of stupidity that Ricky or Lucy had devised.

Fred & Ethel were comically antagonistic towards each other as well.

They rarely accomplished anything good for anyone.

They were buffoons.

They were entertaining to watch in the context of a TV sitcom. But if you knew them in real life, they are people you would likely despise.

They were enablers.

In the clinical sense, enablers are people who help fuel someone's dysfunctional, destructive behavior.

You do not need enablers in your life or in your brand.

So, to help dis-empower Fear & Ego, we let them parade as Fred & Ethel to underscore just how pointless and destructive they can be.

When Fred prevents you from standing for one thing, don't listen to him.

When Ethel tells you, "Yes, I know those are the rules for others, but you're special. And hey, your idea to make quick money selling Vitameatavegamin? Genius!" Don't listen to her.

Remember instead just how little good they've ever accomplished.

Remember just how goofy they really are.

Remember how successful the brands are whose creators stick to the rules with courage and conviction, leaving Fred & Ethel in the dust.

We've seen what happens when people are unable to eschew the siren calls of Fred & Ethel.

Lastly, Fred & Ethel don't exist only in you. They are alive and well in most folks. So when your staff, a neighbor or your aunt's hairdresser bring Fred & Ethel over (and they will), don't let them in.

Everyone will have an opinion about what you're embarking on. These people are often not in the demographic or in any way connected to your business category. And the ones who are, who say things like, "Ya know, I took a marketing class one time and…" Plug your ears and run away. They don't want to help. They want to show you how much they know. That helps you not at all.

BUSINESS OWNERS SELF-DESTRUCT THEIR BRANDS

The unhappy chiropractor in the previous chapter is just one example. It was almost as if he were the evil twin of another chiropractor with whom Blaine had worked. The good guy chiropractor was delightful.

His brand was almost effortless, because he was effortless.

He lived to serve.

He was happy.

He was unafraid, and un-driven by egomania.

The evil twin chiropractor could only think about himself and what he wanted. We don't really know how he ever got as far as he did. He was an unpleasant, snotty man with an inflated ego who, it turned out, left a lot of unpaid bills in his wake.

We've occasionally had a client at Slow Burn who, despite our fairly thorough vetting process, becomes inextricably enmeshed in the clutches of Fred or Ethel.

One such client was a professional activist. He had an advanced medical degree. He'd sold his medical practice in an effort to devote himself to his cause. What he was lacking was a solid brand. For that, he came to us.

In a nutshell: every possible brand we presented was a problem.

Despite what he said he wanted, when confronted with the need to be courageous and commit, he became a squirrel.

During the initial brand presentations, he would enjoy everything that had been brought to the table.

Then, left alone to make a decision, he would return with lengthy email essays detailing the problems with each brand.

Understand, these weren't real problems. They were manufactured objections. In most cases, they were entirely off base and unfounded. And it all came off with an undercurrent of fear...er, Fred. It was as if, when confronted with the reality of the commitment he was making in his professional life, he was mortified. He would then make suggestions that, for reasons we explained to him, would alienate his audience. But they were his ideas and he was falling in love with them. Ego…or, as you've now come to know and love her, Ethel.

We finally said that there was a tone to his communications that suggested maybe he wasn't happy working with us in this process. If he wanted to bail out, we understood; no harm, no foul.

He scrambled for the exit, offering all kinds of rationalizations.

Later on, other professionals we know who'd encountered him had similar experiences. Too bad. He wasn't a bad guy. He just had no control over Fred & Ethel.

It was as if the courage of his activist convictions did not extend to committing to a single potent brand. It made us sad.

All this to say: mustering the nerve to do this properly is an essential quality. None of us is completely immune to victimization at the hands of Fear & Ego. You just need to remember who Fred & Ethel are and beat them down.

So, you feel the fear, you're ready to do it anyway—now what?

Excellent question.

THE FORMULA FOR BRAND WILL SOUND DECEPTIVELY SIMPLE

Like many pursuits, it's not easy to do. It's just easy to say.

And like anything else worth doing that appears effortless, it takes a lot of hard work.

Here now, the basics.

Building a brand requires knowing:

(a) who you are,
(b) who your customer is, and…
(c) where the intersection lies.

Once you understand that, you have to distill the essence that defines your brand.

What could be easier, right?

IGNITION POINTS

- Building a solid brand is rarely easy—typically, it's hard work and takes a while.
- If a brand ever does materialize spontaneously, and it's obviously right, embrace it.
- Beware Fear & Ego: they can derail all your branding efforts.
- Ego will tell you that the rules don't apply to you, which is wrong.
- Fear will tell you the rules can't possibly work, which is also wrong.
- Fear can make you squirrely and prevent any kind of commitment.
- Decisions made from a place of fear are always bad decisions.
- Decisions made from a place of unhealthy ego are always bad decisions.
- As a reminder of how pointless and perilous they can be, remember Fear & Ego as Fred & Ethel.
- Be brave and self-aware enough to recognize who you are, who your customer is, and where the intersection lies.
- If fear intrudes, feel it freely —and go forward anyway.

FIRESTARTER

Time for a little introspection. Think about the times where fear and/or ego have intruded upon life's decisions. Are there any times when your obviously superior ego influenced a decision—only to backfire on you and leave you looking like the cartoon victim of an exploding cigar? How did ego's backfire leave you feeling? How about fear? Think about any instances where you were mortified to move forward—but went ahead anyway, only to find the rewards to be extraordinary. What if you'd listened to the fear instead?

Chapter 9

BRAND: TO THINE OWN SELF BE TRUE

Who are you and why do you do what you do? This is a critical question to be answered in the brand equation.

And you must be honest.

To a point.

That's not to say there's a point where you begin to be dishonest.

But we're talking about defining who you are in relation to your business and your customer.

That means your extraordinary fondness for Hummel figurines probably has no bearing on your brand.

Unless, of course, your business is buying and selling Hummel figurines.

What we're talking about here is persona.

Determining your persona, as it relates to your business, will be defined by answering a three-part question:

1. Who are you?
2. What kind of person are you?
3. What is your chief point of difference?

Think back to the comedians described in Chapter 4. Not one of those people is the person you see on the stage…at least, not completely. The comedian you see on the stage is a persona, a role, a mask. Yes, the persona is based in reality—but an honest and often amplified sliver of reality.

Jeff "You Might Be A Redneck If" Foxworthy plays the good-natured hick. It belies his excellent education and his past career at IBM. Jeff Foxworthy at one time was a professional computer geek.

But Jeff Foxworthy IS from the south.

Jeff Foxworthy DOES seem to have a smattering of redneck in his gene pool.

And Jeff Foxworthy the Private Man is an entirely different person than Jeff Foxworthy the Comedian.

His brand as a comedian is carefully crafted, and based on a persona that represents a small fraction of his personality magnified many, many times—a small fraction that he chose because it was most relevant to his comedy branding.

A business owner, while not in exactly the same situation as a comic, definitely can take something away from this. For a high-profile example, think about Wendy's Hamburgers. The late Dave Thomas was the face of Wendy's for years. His soft-spoken, aw-shucks demeanor and easy smile made him a great brand ambassador.

What you may not know is that Dave Thomas was an orphan. His adoptive mother died when he was 5, and his father traveled the country seeking work. As a teenager, Dave Thomas dropped out of high school to work full-time in a restaurant. Eventually, he became invaluable to Harland Sanders, helping him make Kentucky Fried Chicken a gigantic success through menu and marketing decisions. And by the time Dave Thomas began appearing in Wendy's commercials in the mid-1980s, he didn't even own Wendy's any more.

Most of this has no bearing on the Wendy's brand.

What does matter to the Wendy's brand is Dave Thomas' attitude and philosophy. He was famous at Wendy's for his MBA: "Mop Bucket Attitude." He loved people, he loved restaurants, and he was passionate about delivering high quality. How passionate? Well, you might know that Wendy's was named for his daughter. So he's obviously passionate enough about the business that he put his daughter's name out front. And if you look closely at the Wendy's logo, there's an arc of words above Wendy's head. It says: "Quality Is Our Recipe."

Quality was a big deal to Dave.

Not only is "quality" a permanent part of the Wendy's logo, it's also the first plank in Dave's historical platform of Five Values that serve as a benchmark for Wendy's.

The other four values are Do The Right Thing, Treat People With Respect, Profit Is Not A Dirty Word, and Giving Back.

Do The Right Thing is there because Dave Thomas believed that personal integrity was the single most important value a man can have.

Treat People With Respect is there because Dave Thomas loved people. He believed in treating people the way you want to be treated yourself. His distillation of that is "Just be nice."

Profit Is Not A Dirty Word might seem a bit Gordon Gekko. But this is not a "greed is good" moment. In Dave Thomas's world, far from Gekko's mythical Oliver-Stone Wall Street, turning a profit meant making enough money to share your success, both with your team and with your community.

And Giving Back was a very big deal for Dave Thomas. Sharing your wealth, sure. But also, sharing yourself. Sharing your time. Sharing your talents. And the more you drill down into the Dave Thomas back story, the more you realize how this was such a vital part of who he was.

If you want to know more about Dave, you can go read these Five Values, along with his biography, at the Wendy's website.

What we've seen here is enough to understand how Dave Thomas's persona, integrity first and always, that small slice of his total personality, informed so much about his brand. In fact, it was so crucial to Wendy's success that he was asked to come back as the brand ambassador after he sold the business.

And he's certainly not the first iconic brand leader to find himself in such a position. There have been others, from local to regional to national and international companies where the brand founders have been asked back to represent the brand to both the public and the rank and file.

Would that any of us should be so lucky to sell our business for millions, then make millions more merely by being around.

Now this is not to say you need to become the actual face of your business. It simply serves as a stellar example of how the man's brand is informed by the man himself. We know why Wendy's brand does what it does.

Back to the main point: who are you?

We certainly see who Dave Thomas was.

And we certainly recognize him in the Wendy's brand.

Wendy's might not be as big as #1 McDonald's or #2 Burger King. But Wendy's does run third, and its roots are equally humble. But perhaps the biggest difference is the brand serves as a scalable example for all of us. Dave Thomas' Five Values are just as resonant to one small store as they are to a 6,000-store chain—or a 30,000 store chain.

So who are you? What is your persona?

Why do you do what you do?

Would another example help you deal with these questions?

One from a much smaller business than Wendy's?

TAKE OUR COMPANY. PLEASE.

Blaine Parker is a man who has spent his career working in small business marketing because he loves helping to grow small businesses. It's like sport for him. He's a student of great advertising and legendary ad men. He also spent over a decade working as an Advertising Creative Director at a national radio network—because the one thing he loves about as much as the challenge of growing small businesses is doing it on the radio. (He's also good enough that he's won big national awards doing it. He's the equivalent of an Oscar-winning screenwriter for radio.) Blaine loves solving the advertising puzzle.

Honey Parker is a woman who, for years, lived, breathed and slept Big Agency Advertising. She was, at one time, a Vice President at the world's largest advertising agency. She has worked on Honda, Toyota, Lexus and Mitsubishi. She's worked on DirecTV, Wells Fargo, Toyota, Nerf and Yoo-Hoo. She works with brands who know what it means to "move the needle." A mere 1% uptick in sales can mean millions of dollars in additional revenue. Honey also loves solving the advertising puzzle.

Around the dinner table at the Parker house, the talk is invariably about advertising.

And the challenges.

And the commonalities of the agency/client dynamic, regardless of the size of the agency or the client.

One lovely winter afternoon, when both Blaine and Honey were between full-time gigs, and the sun was shining down on their mountain top, the idea for a business was born.

It would bring big-time advertising agency know-how to small businesses.

Instead of promising instant, flash-in-the-pan results like so many small business advertising experts, this agency would offer slow, realistic, responsible and sustainable growth through strategic branding and implementation.

Although Honey and Blaine knew that small businesses in particular are often looking for flash fires—big results fast—they also knew that this type of marketing burns only briefly, then burns out.

The people Honey and Blaine were talking about working with are real people. People with families and employees, maybe a dog. These weren't faceless corporations. Flash fires are irresponsible. But a slow burn, a sustained fire, now that's reliable. That feeds everyone at the table.

It was determined: their agency would be called Slow Burn Marketing.

They were fine with the fact that the name said right up front: "We aren't going to make huge numbers happen overnight. If that's what you're looking for, you should keep on looking."

Why "marketing" instead of "advertising?"

Because they wanted to be able to address the entire marketing chain, from the name of the company to the way people answer the business's phone to the customer experience.

They also wanted to be able to bring this know-how to business owners who weren't necessarily ready to plunk down the kind of huge retainers required to engage their services. They wanted to be able to offer their knowledge through products that provide useful, actionable information to those who could benefit from it.

They wanted to work with people to change their marketing in ways that can really make a difference in their business.

And Honey and Blaine wanted to work with each other. (CUE MUSIC). It may sound sappy, but winning for a client is even sweeter when it's a group win.

That, in a nutshell, is the essential basis for our company's brand, Slow Burn Marketing.

SO, WHAT'S YOUR STORY?

This is the easiest way to get to the heart of why you do what you do: tell the story that made you get into your business.

Stories are important. They inform and engage. They also force you into a helpful and familiar pattern.

"Once upon a time there was…"

"So I realized I could save the village by…"

"And we all lived happily ever after."

We have a couple of clients whose mission to serve grew out of personal experiences with dire situations. They now provide professional services that are designed to avoid the pitfalls they experienced, thus making other people's lives better.

We have clients whose businesses are not particularly life changing. They do what they do because they have a love for doing it and sharing it with people.

We've seen companies who provide services of a mechanical nature because the owner simply has a love for putting things together. There are manufacturers who are obsessed with making a better product for less.

As you've seen by our example, we do what we do because we love the challenge of it, we love what it can accomplish for people, and it's rewarding to see what happens when marketing is done well.

The Dave Thomas story, as we've seen, is based in loving to serve people a quality product.

If you look at Sir Richard Branson, the man behind the Virgin brand, his stories (he has many) are based in connecting with people, having fun, and setting enormous, seemingly unachievable challenges for himself. From the first Virgin record store to the various Virgin airlines to the Virgin Mobile phone company to the Virgin record labels—all of these business ventures reflect the fun, the connection and the challenge.

You might fancy yourself a wild adventurer like Branson. You might see yourself more as a low-key, Dave Thomas type. You might not see yourself fitting anywhere on that spectrum.

But you have a story.

What is that story?

What event or series of events brought you to where you are now?

What do you love about doing what you do?

In the context of any story you can tell (we hope) there is another person: the customer. That person can literally be "a customer," someone with a problem you solved. Or that person can figuratively be a customer—someone in your life who either was or would have been helped by what you now sell.

We have a client who is an attorney in estate planning and elder law. She saw the extraordinary grief experienced by her own mother upon the death of her father, who had died with no provisions in place whatsoever. She's an attorney specializing in estate planning and elder law because she wants to make sure what happened to her mother never happens to anyone else. That's an honest, honorable mission. And she's feisty about it. Even better. A feisty gal on a mission to make sure seniors can enjoy what they've earned.

Our eye doctor client had eye problems as a child and was helped immeasurably by an excellent eye doctor in his home town. This inspired him to become an eye doctor himself and help other families who are experiencing vision challenges—or better yet, prevent those challenges.

A ski tuner with whom we once worked is obsessed with helping elite athletes ski faster. Having worked on European World Cup tours and tuned skis for Olympic skiers, he now has his own shop where he brings this obsession to anyone interested in skiing faster and better and getting service that's a cut above. In truth, he's a total geek. He's mathematically geeky about eking millimeters of time-saving precision out of a ski's edge. He might even giggle to himself as he does it. We're not sure.

We have a housepainter client. He's a mid-western guy who is also a fine artist. Truly fine. He paints highly detailed portraits and landscapes depicting Native American life. As with many fine artists, the art wasn't paying all his bills. But he's happiest getting paid with a brush in his hand. He enjoys color and how it changes moods.

His joy became making people happier in their own homes. He's not curing cancer. He's not saving vision. He's not even helping Olympians win medals. But every day, he's helping people feel more excited about where they live. He's making them proud to share their homes with others.

That's his story. Even he has one, and it matters in the context of why he paints homes and why the people who hire him recommend him to others.

Notice that not one of these people is in it purely for the money.

That's not a story.

And if it's the only reason you're in your business, we probably can't help you.

But if you're human, if you don't have a heart of stone (something Blaine is often accused of by Honey), you have a real, inspirational reason why you do what you do.

Dig down.

Bring it up.

Look at it from all sides.

Make sure that your story has an emotional component to it. Emotions move people. It's what will move them to your brand.

Be honest: what about this experience really resonates with you and motivated you to take the leap in business that you did?

WHAT KIND OF PERSON ARE YOU?

Are you an amped-up, long-haired, drum-banging, tie-dye wearing, hackey-sack playing, Jerry Garcia lookalike who wants to be the face of your cut-rate used music store? Kind of a post-hippie Crazy Eddie's for previously owned CDs and collectible LPs?

Perfect.

But if you have an accountancy that specializes in serving real estate agents, putting yourself out front as a pitchman looking like that is going to come with some attendant challenges.

All this to say: know what kind of person you are.

Your story and why you do what you do is obviously important.

But you also need to be honest about who you are and where you fit in your own brand. A long-haired, tie-dye wearing, Jerry Garcia lookalike has to know that he can easily be a front man for a music business—but will have trouble being a convincing front man for a business that serves mainstream, suit-wearing professionals. Nothing wrong with having that accountancy. But know yourself relative to your core customer.

Of course, if he has an accountancy that specializes in the medical marijuana trade dispensaries (which now apparently outnumber Starbucks stores in Colorado), that's a different story entirely.

Who you are and how well you can represent your brand are important.

None of this is to say you have to be someone you're not. In fact, that's the last thing we'd recommend. But you do have to know who you are. And if who you appear to be is going to create a disconnect between the brand and the consumer, consider just how much of your persona is going to be on the brand.

For example, take Angie's List. If you're unfamiliar with the company, it's a website that aggregates consumer reviews of local service companies. If you're looking for a plumber, you can join Angie's List and look at how customers rate plumbers in your area. In 2010, Angie's List reportedly had $60 million in revenue, and at this writing is planning an IPO.

With Angie's List, most people have some idea that there's a woman named Angie involved. Her name is Angie Hicks, and she apparently started the company by going door-to-door in Columbus Ohio. She had a 100-square-foot office. If you were an early member of Angie's List, it seems you had to actually call Angie to access the database.

Things have changed a bit since then.

Most people who have heard of Angie's List have never heard of Bill Oesterle. But without Mr. Oesterle, there's a chance Angie's List wouldn't even exist. He's the co-founder and CEO. Angie Hicks interned for Bill Oesterle at a venture capital firm. And if you read Bill Oesterle's bio, he's obviously a financial whiz.

He also isn't the guy you see out in front of the brand.

His personality doesn't really inform the brand.

He's merely the guy who keeps the company running.

The buck stops with Bill Oesterle.

As a co-founder and CEO, Mr. Oesterle is certainly no Richard Branson. He doesn't appear to be flamboyant. He doesn't seem to make world record attempts at balloon flights and ocean crossings. But boy, does he know finance.

As for Angie Hicks, co-founder and Chief Marketing Officer, she doesn't appear to be any Richard Branson, either. She's not out making world record attempts at balloon flights and ocean crossings.

Good thing. Because it wouldn't have much to do with the brand.

But what is significant here is that CMO Angie has a personality that informs the brand. In many ways, she represents the brand's core customer.

The Angie's List brand is very much about Angie Hicks.

Bill Oesterle is the man behind the curtain—but unlike the Great Oz, the levers he pulls actually do something besides belch smoke and thunder. He's immensely important to the inner workings of the company. But the brand is Angie.

We have a client mentioned earlier, a medical wellness clinic called Better. The brand is very much informed by the woman who is the MD and the de facto face of the business. Her core customer is women like her: educated, upwardly mobile, "lady doers."

What most people will never learn about the company is that she is business partners with her husband.

He's a great guy.

He runs the business side of things.

But who he is doesn't inform the brand. That's her domain exclusively.

Dave Thomas certainly wasn't the most glamorous guy—but who he was informed the Wendy's brand in spades. He didn't necessarily need to be the national TV spokesperson. In fact, Clara Peller's "Where's the beef?" lady worked quite well for a while. But Dave Thomas' personality infused everything that happened at that company.

Know who you are, how who you are informs your brand, and how it matters to your core customer.

Back to Slow Burn.

Who are Honey and Blaine and how do their personalities effect the Slow Burn brand? Without going too deep and sounding self-indulgent, they both have a strong, "tough love" side.

"Tough" in that they are on a mission to do what they do correctly for people. "Tough" in that they will not waver or cave. This is business. Your business. Even if you want to muck up the works, they won't let you.

Why?

Because of the "love."

Honey often feels like she's channeling her Jewish mother when she tells a client, "This is for your own good. Now do what I tell you and come give me a hug."

So, how about you?

What kind of person are you?

WHAT'S YOUR CHIEF BRAND DIFFERENCE?

Another incredibly important part of your brand: the Big Difference between you and the competition. It's how you stand apart and become recognized. Without a Big Difference, you're just a me-too company. As Honey likes to say, you're just someone's annoying kid brother. "Hey, me too! I wanna play, too!" At best, me-too companies don't matter. At worst, they're kind of annoying.

Think about the chief brand difference between two distinctly different brands. Walmart is a place for saving money. Target is a place for buying hipper, better stuff for less. The reality? There isn't a huge canyon of actual difference between these two big-box giants. But their brands are distinctly different. And the things that are different about Target—namely, its cooler, hipper products—are what Target hangs its hat on.

Go back to the burger wars for a second. Burger King's chief brand difference is a flame-broiled burger. That's where they stake out their territory. As unemotionally engaging as it is—it's a difference. McDonald's chief brand difference, on the other hand, is about the experience. It's about being the happy place to buy a hamburger. Carl's Jr. is for decadent, napkins-be-damned burger indulgence.

Looking again at a few Slow Burn clients and their chief brand differences, we can start with Dr. Sam's Eye Care. His "straight talk, better vision" brand targeted at Mom grows directly from who he is and what he wants for his patients. And his chief difference is his distinct manner of treating folks. Easy to understand, easy to follow, easy to afford. He could charge more, but he won't. He wants the finest care possible for everyone, without price as a barrier. It's all part of making his services accessible and actionable.

At the medical wellness clinic Better, the chief brand difference is not only that the woman who runs the show is in many ways just like her core patient, but that she's an MD. A lot of the people practicing so-called "wellness" are not MDs. They come from a place of non-medical training. Better makes a difference by combining holistic treatments with proven medical know-how. Better is not merely a wellness clinic, but a medical center for complete living.

We have a Park City realtor client whose chief brand difference is he doesn't actually sell properties in Park City. He doesn't sell multi-million-dollar slope-side homes or resort condos. He sells only off-the-beaten-path real estate in a remote mountain community about seven miles up the road from town. Other realtors try to sell there, but they're never as successful. He outsells all of them dramatically. And the reason is because that's the only area our client concentrates on. He knows all the idiosyncrasies of the place, which has mainly dirt roads, no phone lines, no cable, and many roads are unplowed in the winter. He knows all this because he lives there himself. People joke that he's the unofficial mayor of the subdivision. It's a special place, but it isn't for everyone. His chief brand difference is in knowing. His chief brand difference is in not being a salesman, but a neighbor. His tag line, by the way, is, "Minutes From Park City. Miles From Ordinary." Even at first blush, it sounds more special than buying in Park City.

At Slow Burn Marketing, our chief brand difference is that we bring national advertising experience to small local businesses. Honey spent many, many years working for some of the biggest brands in the world. Blaine has spent many, many years working for small businesses—bringing big advertising philosophy, much of it while employed by a national network. He's also spent many years working as a voiceover talent on national brands. Additionally, both of us have experience in direct response marketing. We've had to pay careful attention to strategy and tactics in an effort to create a measurable response to specific advertising efforts. We've both won national advertising awards for our work. We bring to small business advertising a degree of experience and acumen and philosophy that typically isn't available at this level. We're not for everyone, and that's fine. But we do this because we love it. We love doing work that changes the lives of our clients. But again, our difference is about big agency thinking for small business. Note: this benefits the user.

Your difference can be concrete or more amorphic. You could be the only importer of Italian widgets for 500 miles or you could be the most fun place to get widgets ever (you have a ball pit). Either way, you have to have a difference that customers can clearly point to. And that difference points back to them.

WHO'S YOUR COMPETITION?

Look around you. Who's doing what you're doing? What's their brand? If their brand is well-defined, you have a challenge on your hands. If their brand is less well-defined, defining yours is going to give you an edge. If their brand is non-existent, well…happy day. You have an opportunity.

We've already addressed the notion that me-too brands are a bad idea. An "I wanna be just like them!" brand isn't a brand. It's a weak carbon copy—indefinite, uninspired, easy to ignore.

It's definitely not a good idea to ape the competition.

But it is a good idea to look at the competitors with the strongest brands and see what they're doing so well.

There's also nothing wrong with acknowledging that you're not alone in the marketplace when it comes to telling people why they should pick you. An example of this is an iconic ad campaign from the 1960s. (Don't worry, there's a reason we're going back so far. It matters. Hang on.)

Back in 1963, Hertz was category dominant in the rental car market. They were the 900-pound #1 gorilla of car rental. Avis, a new and tiny competitor, was not. What should they be doing to brand themselves? They clearly couldn't say they were #1. They weren't.

The answer was the classic Doyle, Dane & Bernbach campaign for Avis, "We Try Harder."

Not only does it tell you why Avis is different, it lets you know why you should care. It feels honest and makes you root for them without putting the other guy down. All good things.

Avis branded themselves as the underdog, a strategy that would be anathema to so many A-type business leaders. In the case of Avis, the reason it even happened is because Bob Townsend, then president of Avis, was attracted to the ad agency's maverick reputation. Bill Bernbach is reputed to have said, "OK, we'll do the work, but you have to do exactly what we say."

It's admirable enough that Townsend had the nerve to comply. It's even more admirable that he let the campaign run. In his brilliant, out-of-print volume, *Bill Bernbach's Book*, Bob Levinson points out that surveys showed half the people who saw the ads didn't like them. But the other half did. And, instead of trying to please everyone, they went after the 50% of people for whom the advertising resonated.

But here's something that's key: Avis really did try harder. They lived up to the brand. Executives from Avis and DDB went around the country, talking to Avis employees and explaining to them that the "old Avis try" was now a way of life.

Flash forward to the 21st century: there's a reason you still see various incarnations of that 1963 advertising campaign today. There's also a reason why, at this writing, Avis has been the #1 rental car company for customer loyalty for over a decade according to the Brand Keys Customer Loyalty Engagement Index. And Avis advertising continues to upstage the competition with its "we wanna try harder for you" ethos.

Avis takes a position and sells powerfully against the competition without ever explicitly acknowledging the competition.

So, who's your competition?

How have they defined themselves?

What do they mean to their customers?

How do they make you feel about their brand?

Is their packaging really slick and professional, or is it more low-key and seat-of-the-pants?

When Slow Burn created the brand for Better, the competitors we were up against weren't playing the game in a very upscale way and weren't likely to be medical professionals. The competition was typically more earthy. The branding for Better responds very specifically to that. It has an upscale feel and emphasizes the medical nature of the clinic.

At Dr. Sam's Eye Care, the competition was somewhat old-fashioned and stodgy. In some cases, it wasn't branded well at all, but rather haphazardly and somewhat sloppily. They were certainly all well-intentioned. There simply wasn't any cohesion or focus. By focusing on Mom and sending a defined message relevant to her and her family, the profile of Dr. Sam's Eye Care became significantly elevated—and in some cases actually inspired the competition to up their game.

If you again look around at the burger wars, look at what the big brands are doing. Carl's Jr./Hardees is talking to the experience of young-adult burger decadence. McDonald's is a happy burger experience. Burger King is a flame-broiled burger. If you were coming into the marketplace against these three, how would you respond? How would you differentiate yourself from them? Hint: saying, "I'm the happier, flame-broiled, decadent burger experience" might not be the right answer—which takes us to our next question…

ARE YOU DIFFERENT ENOUGH?

This can be a serious challenge. Because let's face it: sometimes, you're doing business in a commodity marketplace. Sometimes, there's virtually no difference between what you're selling and what the competition is selling. You have the exact same stuff.

What then?

We've already discussed the Target Factor. How much of a grand difference is there between shopping at Walmart and shopping at Target? Not a whole lot, when you get right down to it. But there are people who love Target who wouldn't be caught dead in Walmart. That's because, despite their similarities, Target has done an excellent job of positioning its brand difference. It's the hipper, more fun alternative to Walmart.

How about coffee? Talk about a commodity product. But there are people who swear by their Starbucks. Others swear by their Peet's, and would never switch. Peet's definitely has a certain higher-end snob appeal that even Starbucks doesn't quite reach for. But let's put the more recent, high-end coffees aside for a moment.

Let's look at a brand somewhat more prosaic.

For decades, Folgers has been "Mountain Grown."

For years, there were TV commercials bragging about the fact that Folgers is "richer because it's mountain grown."

And remember, this started back in the mid-1960s. For over 20 years on TV, Mrs. Olsen reminded viewers that Folgers is "mountain grown, the richest kind of coffee." While Mrs. Olsen has left us, the claim remains stamped on the side of every can of Folgers coffee.

Do you know where most coffee grows?

In the mountains.

In fact, if you've ever seen *Out of Africa* starring Meryl Streep as Karen Blixen, you might remember when she wanted to start a coffee plantation, she was told that the her property was at too low an elevation.

Yes, as all you coffee fanatics out there know, robusta coffee will grow at lower altitudes. It also comprises a minority of coffee crops and tastes nasty. The vast majority of coffee is Arabica and is—by default—mountain grown.

That certainly didn't stop Folgers from setting themselves apart in a commoditized, packaged-goods marketplace by proclaiming their "difference." Or, in this case, their "special." Special because it's mountain grown. Even though it's not really so special but pretty much standard.

If there's a similar quality between you and all your competitors, but nobody's talking about it, is it possible to claim it as your own?

It is, but you have to say it first and commit big. You can't whisper it. So then, anyone who tries to follow is just a "me too" kid brother.

While it's not his brand, but part of his advertising, an example of this is Dr. Sam. He offers "free eye exams for infants." This is a service offered by many, many eye doctors. It's part of a program from the American Optometric Association called InfantSEE. Optometrists volunteer free eye exams for children.

But none of the two dozen other InfantSEE volunteers in Dr. Sam's vicinity are talking about it.

He is.

Therefore, he owns that idea.

Again, we're talking about an advertising tactic versus a brand differentiation. But the concept is similar.

If it's nearly impossible to truly be different, find something you can claim as "special"—something that matters without sounding contrived. As disingenuous as it might seem on the face of it, "Mountain grown" really has powerful implications for the consumer. It sounds difficult and expensive, so it must be better. It paints a positive picture. If you were really tuned in to coffee, you knew that the market had seen an influx of low-elevation robusta beans during World War II, and it hadn't necessarily gone away. Mountain grown is made into a proprietary uniqueness—but simply because they said it first. It's effective nonetheless. Since Folgers claimed it, nobody else can do the same. And it resonates with consumers.

ARE YOU AFRAID TO COMMIT?

If so, save yourself. Get out now.

Really.

Commitment is critical. If you can't commit to your brand, if you can't embrace it, if you want to flip-flop and be wishy-washy, then you're doomed in this process.

In doing this, you're going to have to risk the disapproval of others. And there will be disapproval. One of the directives we give new clients is that, during the branding process, they MUST NOT show where things are going to anyone else. All it will do is invite disapproval and create doubt. Fred & Ethel are everywhere. Fear & Ego abound, and everyone's happy to share the pain with an unsuspecting client in the midst of brand building. And in the end, it will completely undermine any possible commitment to the brand.

Early on, before we gave this directive to clients, we had one say to us, "Well, my mother-in-law says—"

And we had to stop the discussion.

Because if you're going to make branding decisions based on something your mother-in-law says, you're asking for trouble. She's not in marketing, she's probably not your core customer, and even if she is, the interpersonal dynamic is simply incorrect for making these decisions.

You have to know in your heart that what you're doing is the right thing. Do you remember the title of this chapter? "Brand: To Thine Own Self Be True."

This is about living an authentic life, and bringing your authentic self to the brand. It means you're willing to risk the disapproval of others to live your life.

And, as we all know, you're never going to please all of the people all of the time.

When your brand is a success, you'll be amazed at how quickly the naysayers "loved it all along."

You need only please your core customer.

So know who you are. Be committed, be courageous, be brave, be yourself—and good things happen.

IGNITION POINTS

- Be completely candid and honest: who are you relative to your business?
- Your values, your ethics, your attitude and your philosophies about business are all key factors in your brand—though not necessarily THE brand.
- How do you want to honor and serve your customer?
- How does what you love doing matter?
- Is there anything about your personal story that informs your brand?
- What kind of a person are you?
- At all costs, avoid being a "Me Too" brand, which is essentially a business version of someone's annoying little brother.
- You are obligated to stake out a territory that's different from your competitors.
- If you truly, honestly have no difference, if you're a commodity, follow the Folger's "Mountain Grown" coffee example: stand out by claiming common but otherwise unrecognized territory as your own.
- If you can be the first to claim a commonality and make it yours, you own it.
- You must be authentic, because it's difficult to commit to fakery, and customers can see through it.
- Beware Fred & Ethel, who loom large through this process.

FIRESTARTER

If possible, think about three brands that you would consider to be "Me Too" brands—businesses whose identities aren't linked to anything honest, but are merely aping the competition. How much respect do you have for those businesses? Now, think about three brands you know that you would consider authentic reflections of the person at the top. How do you feel about those brands? Are there any cues you can take from these three businesses in building your own brand?

Chapter 10

WHO'S BUYING YOU?

So, you've defined who you are, why you do what you do and why you're different from your competition. It's time to define your customer. You need to know three things:

1. Who are they?
2. What is their biggest fear about what you do?
3. Where will they find their joy?

DEMOGRAPHICALLY YOURS

If you're like most business owners, you're going to hate this part. Ready?

You have only one customer.

Yes, one.

There is one core customer who typifies the market you cater to.

Who is your core customer?

What are they about?

What is going on in their lives?

This doesn't mean you can't serve others. The core customer at Dr. Sam's Eye Care is "Mom."

That doesn't mean unmarried men can't be subject to the appeal of Dr. Sam.

Plenty of men are.

But Mom is the identifiable core customer.

Mom informs the brand, the message, and the entirety of the persona Dr. Sam's presents to the public.

It's helped make Dr. Sam a local celebrity.

Would you like to enjoy celebrity status, or otherwise make your business an iconic, category-dominant juggernaut?

You need ONE identifiable core customer.

Yes, there may be many different types of people who would patronize your business. But you have to pick one identifiable person to whom you're going to speak.

If only one perfect customer were ever going to patronize your business ever again, what would he or she look like?

Male or female?

How old?

What does he or she do for a living?

How about hobbies?

What kind of car?

What kind of home?

What education level?

Do they have children?

Income?

Sophistication level?

How about pets?

If this customer has a free hour, what does he or she do?

What do they watch on TV?

Are they spending discretionary income with you? If so, what else might they buy instead of what you're selling?

If this purchase is a necessity, who else might they buy it from?

How does this customer see him- or herself?

This might seem overly detailed and trivial. It's not.

Consider this.

Once upon a time, Blaine worked for a business that sold high-end audio and video equipment. The man for whom he worked had been running this business for over 20 years. And in those two decades, his customer base had shifted considerably.

For example…

When the business opened in the early '70s, it was catering to a 20-something male.

This 20-something male was probably a young professional whose hobby was partying. He probably drove an imported coupe or a sports car. He likely lived in a rental apartment. He was a college graduate who made a decent income, but wasn't rich. He considered himself worldly and read *Rolling Stone* magazine. He likely had no pets. If he had a free hour, he'd probably listen to music and drink a couple of beers before going out with his girlfriend. He was spending discretionary income, for sure. If he didn't buy audio equipment, he might buy a motorcycle instead. If he bought it someplace else, it might come from a similar store about a mile up the street or from a large discount store that sold on price instead of quality. This guy saw himself as sophisticated (even if he wasn't), social, witty, and going places. His biggest fear about buying audio equipment would be that he's buying the wrong thing. He'd want to go into the deal informed, making sure it was powerful enough to deliver the volume and the punch he was looking for, and that it would be prestigious enough to impress his friends.

That's the guy who was buying audio equipment from this dealer in the 1970s. Knowing these details informed the product line and the sales approach.

In the 1990s, things had changed considerably.

The business was no longer catering to that core customer. The base had shifted.

Instead, the store was catering to a 40-something male. He was a middle-aged professional whose hobby was golf. He drove a German import. He lived in a decent-sized house. He was a white collar professional making six figures. He still considered himself worldly, but read *Newsweek* instead of *Rolling Stone*. He had a dog and a cat.

If he had a free hour, he'd probably do some yard work or spend time with the kids. He was spending discretionary income—but more of it. If he didn't buy audio equipment, he might buy a new car instead. If he bought the equipment someplace else, it still might come from a similar store about a mile up the street or from a large discount store that sold packages deals. This guy saw himself as sophisticated (and was), social, witty, and instead of going places, had arrived. His biggest fear about buying audio equipment would be that he was buying the wrong thing. He'd want to go into the deal informed, making sure it was powerful enough to deliver the volume and the punch he was looking for, that it would be prestigious enough to impress his friends—and that it would be easy enough for his wife and kids to operate. It also probably included TV and home theater audio instead of just a stereo system for music playback.

And you know what all that means?

It means a completely different product mix and sales approach than for the 1970s customer. It also means a completely different brand image.

The 1970s core customer rocked and rolled.

The 1990s core customer kicked back and had a cocktail.

The 1970s core customer was about long hair.

The 1990s core customer was about expensive shoes.

The 1970s core customer was about sex.

The 1990s core customer was about family.

So, does this mean that in the 1970s, a middle-aged family man who wanted an easy-to-operate system for his family couldn't shop there? Of course not. Just like the 1990s brand didn't mean a long-haired, heavy-metal, knuckle-dragger couldn't shop there. But that's not who the store was designed for in either decade.

But the core customer was still key in defining the brand.

Just like McDonald's core customer might be a mom with a kid, Honey and Blaine (who are middle-aged marketing jetsetters without kids) still have no compunction about stopping in for a quick bite alongside a group of teenagers from the local high school. (Well… maybe Honey does.)

THE CORE CUSTOMER DEFINED IS A TOOL—NOT AN EXCLUSION

Just as an example, let's look at a brand that is absolutely defined as a product for one well-defined core customer—yet is used by another customer who in all ways completely defies that definition.

Ever heard of Pedialyte?

In the US, this product is probably the #1 brand of oral electrolyte solution to replace fluids and minerals after diarrhea and vomiting in babies and small children. It's marketed to moms. "Pedialyte helps kids feel better fast!"

The brand is pretty solid if grammatically questionable.

Yet, something has happened.

Its kid-intended, mom-centric branding hasn't stopped any number of marathon runners or any of the pro athletes on the Arizona Cardinals, Anaheim Ducks, Chicago Bears, the Atlanta Braves or the New York Mets from using Pedialyte instead of Gatorade. Athletes like Pedialyte for its rehydration potential. It promotes quick fluid and electrolyte absorption, and has much less sugar than sports drinks.

The core customer is mom. That's not going to change.

But there's no electric fence around the brand telling big hairy men to stay out.

MAN, WOMAN OR KID?

If you could ever only have one more customer come to you, who would it be? Define your core customer in detail. Defining this customer will inform your brand and all your subsequent marketing.

It's highly unlikely the Harry Potter brand was ever designed for anyone over the age of 16, but millions of adults have happily flocked to it and become fanatical about it.

The Trader Joe's core customer is an "unemployed college *professor* who drives a very, very used *Volvo*." It would be difficult to operate 358 stores nationwide with an annual revenue of over $8 billion if the only people shopping there were unemployed college professors driving old Volvos.

The core customer is not a lockout device. The core customer helps give you a direction and a voice. The core customer is a defining element. Embrace the idea of your core customer.

And be sure you like doing business with them. It makes a difference.

FEELING THEIR FEAR

You've defined your core customer to a T. Now, get ready for defining a motivation you may never have considered: what is his or her biggest fear about the product or service you sell?

Yes, fear.

Fear is one of the most important emotions to consider relative to your customer. That's because fear is what keeps people on the fence and off of your balance sheet.

FEAR IS GOOD FOR BUSINESS

We're using fear as a defining element not because we want to induce fear, as so many sales psychologists of a certain stripe would like you to do. You'll frequently hear from sales gurus that fear is a powerful motivator. And there are certainly times when fear has its place in an advertising message. But, where brand is concerned, we don't want to look so much at scaring people as understanding them and speaking to them.

We need to define the fear because it helps us understand the core prospect's motivations—especially what prevents them from buying from us. Fear can cause paralysis. People may buy because you touch their heart. They may also stay away because something somewhere has triggered their fear.

That fear could be something like, "I'm afraid that Lasik surgery will leave me with two smoking holes where my eyes used to be." A big fear and possibly worth speaking to. It's a tall order for a brand, but worth taking into consideration.

The fear could be as mundane as, "If I shop there, people will think I'm a dork." Not such a big fear. But still possibly worth speaking to.

With Avis, almost half a century after they began claiming to be "#2 and trying harder," the brand is now indirectly speaking to the fear that customer service at car rental companies often sucks. The brand is promising that they're going to bend over backwards to make sure you drive away happy. (Trust us: as frequent rental car customers, we've abandoned the discount car rental companies for the slightly more expensive rates and vastly better service at Avis.)

When we re-branded the Susan Graham Law Office as Senior Edge Legal, we were speaking directly to senior citizens who don't have a plan in place. Estate planning is an area where fear keeps people from acting. By implying that the firm's specific goal is to give seniors an edge in their affairs, it speaks directly to that fear of the unknown and assuages it with the notion that the goal is specifically to give you a leg up. "Law office" is amorphous and scary. "Senior Edge" is pretty specific and has a benefit built in. From the moment the firm changed its name, clients began affirming that they understood and appreciated the meaning.

Taking that fear into account, we can then speak to those motivations in more meaningful ways.

FEAR, MEET HAIR

For example, we've previously discussed our hair salon client. This is not an enormously life-changing service.

It is, however, a service fraught with emotional challenges when it comes to the prospect's ego.

One need only look at the plethora of signs on hair salons that say "We fix $8 haircuts" to begin to understand the challenges. Nobody wants a lousy haircut. And if you've ever watched the TV series *What Not To Wear*, where people who dress horrendously are given makeovers, you know what happens when it comes to the stylist's chair: many of these *What Not To Wear* participants are unable to part with whatever hairstyle they have, regardless of how awful it might be.

The core challenge usually involves some manner of self-definition, often connected to the length of their hair. It would require years of intensive therapy to get these people past the problem of self-identity through hairstyle. And the irony is, the *What Not To Wear* stylists typically do fabulous work. They send their subjects away looking extraordinary. But there is a deep and pervasive current of social anxiety disorder related to haircuts. In extreme cases, it requires the assistance of a mental health professional.

So, haircut fear is an established fact.

Many, many people find choosing a salon frustrating.

There's an entire spectrum of intensity for this frustration, from mild annoyance to utter paralysis.

And it's just a haircut.

Yet, once you know this, you can then do something about it. You can hit the nail on the head if it's a fairly concrete problem such as, "We fix $8 hair cuts." (How many little, otherwise unbranded salons have put out that sign?)

Or, you can talk to the person in a way that lets them know you're on their side and have a sense of humor and joy about your hair challenges, such as in Ooh La La's "Love, Truth, Hair."

Both approaches let the customer know that you understand them. It also opens the door, invites them in, and lets you start to sell to them.

FEAR, MEET VISION

To step up the intensity of the fear factor, look at Dr. Sam's Eye Care. The core customer defined is Mom.

What is Mom's fear about choosing an eye doctor? That she's going to choose the wrong one.

Especially in an age of often abysmal managed care, when stories of short shrift and malpractice abound, Mom does not want the wrong eye doctor.

She wants an eye doctor who knows what he's talking about, is thorough, and is sensitive to the requirements, both medical and emotional, of her and her children. She doesn't want to stand on the sidelines out of control. She wants to understand what's happening to her child. She wants professional help and guidance. And she doesn't want to pay through the nose.

FEAR, MEET THE PROSPECT OF DEATH

Taken to the far end of the spectrum, when someone is given a positive diagnosis of cancer, they feel alone and confused.

The One to One, "It's personal" brand speaks directly to the heart and head of a scared, confused and possibly even desperate prospect.

They're afraid they could die.

They're afraid of choosing the wrong doctor.

They're afraid of any number of possible outcomes.

FEAR, MEET THE FRIVOLOUS

Let's face it: not everyone's business is about earth-shaking, emotionally profound buying decisions.

McDonald's and Burger King and Carl's Jr. don't sell anything that changes anyone's life. They sell a diversion.

What's the fear factor there?

The fear that I'm going to get a lousy hamburger?

The fear that my kids aren't going to be happy at mealtime?

The fear that I won't impress my friends with my choice of fast food?

And here's a thought: have these brands defined themselves so well that they've created a fear? The fear that comes with leaving your chosen burger club. Some people actually define themselves by which burger place they select. Even though they're only regional, many folks across this great nation of ours have heard about In-N-Out Burger. Fans of In-N-Out are rabidly loyal to the core. As a competitor, what are you going to do to get prospects to set aside the fear that going to your burger place will not be a wasted opportunity to revel over a double double, monster style? (Want to talk about a brand club? In-N-Out even has its own underground, not-on-the-menu ordering slang.) We would posit that Carl's Jr./Hardees has done quite a good job of encroaching on In-N-Out's territory—and their products are more widely available. They've done a fine job of alleviating the potential fear that you might not get your full burger on.

Now, as fears, these certainly aren't worries that tip the scale against a young adult's haircut phobia, a senior's estate planning, a child's eyesight, or a woman's cancer treatment.

But they are little, mundane, daily challenges that motivate people to make buying decisions—or no decision. And, taken in isolation, a single five-dollar buying decision doesn't really impact anyone's business. But taken in aggregate, millions of five-dollar buying decisions are serious needle movers.

As we said, these are not world-changing fears. Nonetheless, by addressing these fears, they inform a brand image that becomes solid and identifiable. Which leads us to the final part of the fear-meets-brand equation...

HAPPY, HAPPY, JOY, JOY

Next on the hit list—joy.

We know who they are, whether they watch *Nova* or *Dancing With The Stars*. We know what keeps them up at night, as well as the little vanities they'd never admit to in public. But where will they find the joy in what you're offering? It's the "What's in it for me" portion of the equation.

Now that you know them, do you know what it is about what you do that will curl their toes, bathe them in relief, want to hug you, get them thinking about baking you cookies?

That last one has been known to happen.

(We've had at least one client bake us a pie.)

PRIDE AND JOY

Joy can come in many forms. For years the Home Depot has hung their hat on the pride that comes with a job well done. Whether using the tag line "You can do it. We can help" or the newer "More Saving. More Doing," a key component of their message has been look how good you'll feel (*feel*) when you can stand back and see what you've accomplished. "Look what you're capable of. We believed in you all along." That's pretty potent stuff.

Slow Burn Marketing has done work for a local house painter. For him, knowing his audience meant knowing that he was dealing with a lot of second home owners. His core customer was the wife in these families. She has money. She entertains often. Her home is a show place. She sees everything in it as a reflection on her. For his business, the tag line "It's not just paint. It's how you look" elevated his offering and his brand.

He isn't going to just come in and paint your walls. He's going to create something you'll be proud of. He's going to make you excited to throw that next cocktail party and show off your home. Also, subliminally, he is seeding the thought that you may not be looking your best at the moment. He can help change that.

This is a very different message from a painter who is going to help you find your joy by spending a few bucks to paint your house so you can sell it for the most money possible. He's not working on pride. He's aimed at relief.

OH WHAT A RELIEF IT IS

In the category of joy stemming from relief, Alka-Seltzer set the bar way back when. It started with Speedy. A character with a human head, arms and legs, and an Alka-Seltzer tablet for a body. He was there to speed relief to the indigestion sufferer. The promise of fast relief. If you've ever suffered from heartburn, you know how uncomfortable it can be. Speedy results from a friendly little guy. I'll take it.

Then came the jingle "Plop, plop, fizz, fizz. Oh, what a relief it is." It was everywhere. You're probably humming it right now. Don't worry; it will pass in a few hours. Viewers were shown a succession of people demonstrating the opening of the package, the fizzing in the glass, the drinking and…the relief.

Much relief, if it doesn't come in the form of relief from pain or discomfort, is found in the form of stress relief. We're human. We have a lot of stress. It literally shortens lives. If you can help someone relax about something that's even a minor stress, you will probably earn a fan. To that end, there are some types of stress that come in the form of travel, like renting a car. Back in the '80s, and '90s, Alamo Rent A Car ran a series of TV commercials that were pure poetry. Voiced by the ad agency's namesake, Hal Riney, these commercial told stories. Stories about driving. Each commercial would pick a different stretch of road somewhere in the U.S. and paint a picture. For instance, take this particular 30 second spot from 1990 featuring beauty shots of sunshine, oceans and beaches, and happy, laughing people doing things in the water, and oh, yes, the incidental shot of a shiny, late-model rental car amid the action. Hal Riney's soothing, Morning in America voice says:

> It's almost as if someone once said, "Just in case people like sunshine and water, we better make Florida. And we better make miles of beautiful beaches, and places like St. Augustine and Key West, just in case people want to go to them." There are over 4 million miles of roads in Alamo territory, all across America. And nationwide, only Alamo gives you all those miles for free. Including the ones that run through a state that's named after sunshine.

Ahhhh. Both Blaine and Honey have spent time living in Florida and visiting there as well. Neither of us has ever seen a Florida as glorious and stress-free as the Florida of Alamo Country. And as icing on the cake, "…all the miles are free." Without ever saying "We know renting a car is stressful," without ever talking about how you might stress about going over your mileage limit, Hal Riney created advertising for Alamo that was stress relieving. Alamo became the antidote to rental car stress.

And speaking of antidotes and the 80's, Club Med ran a hugely successful campaign, billing itself as "The antidote to civilization." They could have said, "Hey, look how much fun you'll have here." But they knew their audience was a bunch of stressed-out yuppies who spent way too much time on the treadmill of life. They just needed to let go. To stop. Club Med gave them permission…oh, and a beach.

THE PLEASURE OF GUILTY PLEASURE

Indulge. Come on. It's okay. Joy often finds itself in the permission to cross a line that you know you shouldn't. Whether it's a pint of rich, chocolate Häagen-Dazs with a ribbon of creamy caramel running through it or a low calorie substitute, the message is, it's okay to enjoy. A lot of food products, particularly desserts, take this path. And it's a strong motivator. But, how might a guilty pleasure show up in other categories?

Let's travel back to our comedians. We talked about Lisa Lampanelli, Andrew Dice Clay and even Don Rickles. All three of these comedians say things that you shouldn't say in polite company. They may even be saying things that you had already thought, or wished you could say. And what they do is create an environment where it's safe to admit to enjoying the fact that somebody actually went there.

For many years DirecTV ran a campaign known as, "Feel The Joy." It was over-the-top fun based on the premise of how people who love television are overcome with emotion when the DirecTV installer puts in their new system. Generally, our culture says that watching a lot of television is a bad thing. Yet statistics show that most Americans do it…a lot. DirecTV decided to embrace the guilty pleasure and celebrate the behavior. And people loved the advertising. They called DirecTV.

To take it a step further, Honey actually worked on direct marketing for DirecTV's NFL Sunday ticket. If television viewers can be obsessive, football fanatics are… well, more fanatic. You know these guys. (And if you're from the South, you know these gals.) For them, DirecTV spoke right to the heart of their guilty pleasure in a way that not only said it was OK, but got right in your face. The headline that made the client most nervous? "On Sundays all my friends are named, Shut Up."

JOY TO THE WORLD

There are many more ways for someone to find their joy in what you do. Joy can be big, small; it can be life changing or just let someone mark one thing off their considerable list. Are you helping someone feel good about themselves, or removing an obstacle so they can go after what they really want?

You need to know who you're talking to, what problems they face and what the effect of you solving those problems will have on them.

Remember, joy is an emotion. You feel it. Just thinking about how you are going to make someone feel as a result of what you do puts you many steps ahead of most businesses.

These aren't just the facts, ma'am.

Facts don't move people.

Joy moves people…right to your door.

IGNITION POINTS

- Who is your single core customer, and what is he or she all about?
- In defining your core customer, it's helpful to use Trader Joe's as a model: their core customer is an "unemployed college professor who drives a very, very used Volvo."
- Defining your core customer does not prevent other people from patronizing you, any more than Pedialyte targeting moms of infants prevents athletes from buying Pedialyte as a sports nutrition product.
- What is your core customer's single biggest fear about buying what you sell?
- How does your brand meet and address that fear—without flat out saying, "We know you're scared of this."
- Is the fear about an issue of deep consequence, or is it a minor or even insignificant fear?
- Where is your core customer's joy relative to what you sell?
- Is your core customer's joy a minor and fleeting joy, like eating a burger, or a life-changing joy, like being treated well in a battle with cancer?
- Understanding fears and joys is key—they are emotions linked to your brand, and emotions (not facts) are what motivate people to act.

FIRESTARTER

Define your single core customer's life as if you were writing a short biography about him or her. Then, list all the fears this customer harbors about making a purchase from a business like yours. After the fears, list all the potential joys this core customer can experience by using the product or service you sell. How do they feel their fear, and how do they feel the joy?

Chapter 11

FEAR AND JOY AT THE INTERSECTION OF YOUR BRAND

As we know, fear prevents people from acting. Part of the job of your brand is to help prospects get past the fear. If your brand can make your prospect feel the right thing, you're on your way to winning friends and influencing people—people you will be able to call customers.

So, to find the intersection, you must answer the following questions:

1. Why does what you love matter to your prospect?
2. How you will get your prospect past their fear?
3. How do you want them to feel when they leave you?

In answering the first two questions, you find where those two qualities—their fear and your joy—come together in a way that makes the fearful feel not so afraid. In other words, why does what you love doing matter enough to your customer that they'll put fear aside and come to your door...pick up the phone...visit your website...?

How do you get them past their fear?

How does it make their life better?

Last, but certainly not least, is: how do you want them to feel when they leave your business? This is the message they are going to take with them out into the world. It's not only why they'll come back, but why they'll bring new prospects with them.

And remember, it's entirely possible that when we say fear, we're talking about an extremely low-grade fear that doesn't necessarily change anyone's life. It merely prevents them from making a buying decision today.

Choosing where to buy a hamburger today isn't exactly an earth-shaking decision. But it could be motivated out of fear—the fear that I don't know if I'm going to get a lousy hamburger.

We've certainly driven past the as-yet-untried local hamburger joint and had a conversation like, "Want a burger?"

"I dunno. Ya think it's any good?"

"I haven't ever heard anyone say anything about it."

"It could suck."

"True."

"Let's just eat at home."

"OK."

Fear of getting a lousy burger isn't changing our lives in any meaningful way.

But it could be changing the life for the owner of that burger joint.

Because his brand is weak, he's never made us feel anything about his brand, and there's no emotional reassurance of any kind that we're going to be happy about the 15 or 20 bucks we end up spending in his business.

If his brand worked harder—wait, scratch that.

If he actually had *any brand at all*, there's a much better chance that he'd get us to make a choice. As it is, his name, his signage, the appearance of his business, none of it is in any way calculated to make us feel anything.

Well, it might make us feel one thing: apathy.

And a prospect who feels nothing is going to do nothing, relative to making a purchasing decision.

WHAT ARE YOU PEDDLING?

Let's consider a hypothetical to see how this works. There's a bike store in town. Nothing fancy. Just a nice, "conveniently located" bike store with "a friendly, well-trained staff."

Yes, the old "friendly, well-trained staff."

So what?

Who cares?

Why go to them?

Their "convenient location?" That is (a) entirely subjective, and (b) meaningless as a sales point. (No place people have to drive out of their way for is conveniently located. Conversely, it's "worth the drive.")

Let's quickly put this bike store through the brand mill.

What does what Mr. Bike Store love?

Well, the owner loves getting kids riding a two-wheeler for the first time. He enjoys the feeling of accomplishment that comes with it—both for himself and for the kid who rides for the first time. He knows that this accomplishment will help build confidence for a child—confidence that the child can then take into life. The reason he knows it is because as a kid, he had challenges with coordination. It took him much longer than the other kids to master a bike. He wouldn't accept any help. He'd just get on his bike every day after school and push it along with his feet back and forth in front of the house. Then one day, he came bursting into the family kitchen and announced that he could ride. His mother cried.

So now we know what Mr. Bike Store loves.

Why does what he loves matter to his prospect?

Well, his prospect is Dad. Dad handles the majority of sporting equipment purchases for the family. And Dad's joy comes from a similar place as the owner's joy. He enjoys seeing his kid accomplish life benchmarks like catching a ball, fishing for trout, riding a bike. He will also brag about it to his friends. Hey, he's Dad.

Next, what is dad's fear and how will the owner get him past it?

Dad fears that his kid will give up on the bike before he learns how to ride it. Maybe his kid is a chubby, video-game playing closet dweller.

Maybe he has a short attention span and has been known to give up quickly. Maybe he won't like the color and secretly wants a pink bike with unicorn decals. If, for whatever reason, his child fails to ride the bike, then Dad has failed on some level as well.

How's that for a fear?

So, being a savvy guy, the bike store owner offers a 90-day money-back guarantee. "For whatever reason, if your kid doesn't like the bike, you have 90 days to return it, no questions asked."

Wow.

That's big.

How can Dad go wrong?

And you know what? No dad is ever coming back after 90 days to say, "My kid can't ride the darn thing. I want my money back."

Finally, what does Mr. Bike Store want Dad to feel when he leaves?

Easy. He wants Dad to feel like he cares about his kid as much as Dad does. And that's not hard, because he does. He comes from a place of honesty (as should you and every other business owner looking to build a brand). And Dad will tell all the other dads about Mr. Bike Shop, and the world will be safe for kids to learn how to ride bikes.

Does this work in the real world?

Sure.

Read on.

FEELING THE JOY WHERE FEAR MEETS YOUR HEAD

As we've already noted, choosing a new hair stylist can be a decision that rests on a broad spectrum of fear. From the low-grade, "I don't know what I'm gonna get" fear of trying a new hair stylist to the abject mortification of "My hair defines me and I'd rather die than get it cut," it's difficult to imagine something which, when you get right down to it, is more technically mundane than a haircut.

Really, think about it: it's a pair of scissors meeting a bunch of dead cells.

But the social ramifications of what those scissors can do to those dead cells has such extraordinary potential, we have that fear spectrum.

What do we do about it?

Obviously, we can't do anything about the people who need a psychologist.

But we can help instill confidence in our client's prospect by being disarming.

The Ooh La La hair salon brand uses humor and engaging iconic imagery to help the prospect get past the frustration of making a choice.

Look at the tag line: "Love, Truth, Hair."

It's difficult to take that too, too seriously. There's definitely a tongue-in-cheek element to it. At the same time, there's a bit of poignancy. It might make you laugh. But in its silliness and its touch of parody, it inspires you to let your guard down. The ideas of love and truth definitely have something to recommend them. The brand welcomes you with humor.

Combined with its hipster winged-heart, tattoo-ish logo, and the humorous, hair-fun advertising, the brand touches both the heart and the head. (No pun intended. Really.)

Understand, we're not talking about this brand as if it were great art. It's not like being captivated by *Mona Lisa* or being immersed in the extraordinary, head- and heart- bending experience of one of Cristo's epic environmental installations, like gift-wrapping the German Reichstag or filling New York's Central Park with more than 7,000 gates made of flowing, saffron colored fabric.

But Ooh La La's brand does, in its own humble way, engage the prospect.

The brand helps put him or her off their guard enough to get them past their fear and into the stylist's chair. Part of Ooh La La's marketing comes in the form of online videos, which are kind of like little TV commercials. And they're designed specifically to engage and put the viewer just a little off their guard. Each video is one person talking about their real experience in the stylist's chair with honesty and a bit of a self-effacing wink. We never see the people, only their words in type on the screen as they say them. This takes down specific visual barriers (like one person's specific style) and lets the viewer project themselves into the piece.

Once they've engaged Ooh La La, their lives are presumably better because they have a better haircut…or better hair color…or a better eyelash extension (yeah, that's a new one for us, too).

No, their lives aren't better in a way that suddenly having a multi-million-dollar trust fund might make it better.

But on the relatively low end of the scale, where daily happiness lives, better hair is a good thing.

When that customer leaves Ooh La La, they need to feel like they made the right choice. We want them to feel more attractive. And we want them to share the love, the truth, and (yes) the hair. And for anyone who doubts the significance of feeling good about your appearance, again: just watch a few episodes of *What Not to Wear*. It's an extraordinary ad hoc social laboratory. These people's lives change significantly because they stop dressing like slobs, get better hair (at least the ones who aren't completely obstinate and insist on defining themselves by whatever un-styled mass of dead cells is hanging down to their waist), and start taking pride in their appearance.

FEELING THE JOY WHERE FEAR MEETS YOUR EYES

When it comes to eye care, the "Straight Talk, Better Vision" ethos of Dr. Sam's Eye Care speaks directly to Mom's fear about choosing the wrong eye doctor.

By itself, "Straight Talk, Better Vision" might be just a tag line.

But, when you consider that Dr. Sam's joy is in being an eye geek and imparting his knowledge, and that he loves taking the time to teach, and teach well, and make himself clearly understood, well, that's something else. He's not about impressing folks with how much he knows. It's about giving them a new and valuable understanding of their vision.

We're also in an age when the public distaste for managed care is at an all-time high. Doctors often have less time to be human and caring. Additionally, many doctors simply don't know how to speak in a way patients can comprehend. With so many obstacles to feeling good about health care, Dr. Sam's straight talk is a welcome antidote.

When combined with Dr. Sam's folksy, conversational and easygoing advertising messages, and his obvious knowledge and proficiency, the Dr. Sam brand becomes disarming enough to let Mom consider making that phone call.

And once she does, and she begins working with Dr. Sam, she feels good about the experience, knows that her family is in good hands, and has one less thing weighing on her mind. When Mom leaves Dr. Sam's, she feels like she's gotten reliable information, good care, and she's paid a fair price. Mom leaves feeling good about the experience and trusting Dr. Sam. And what the good doctor then sees is Mom making appointments for her entire family. It happens. Patients have said things like, "I loved this so much, I'm bringing all five of my boys!"

FEELING THE JOY—IMPOSSIBLE?

Joy is all relative. It's probably not the exact word you want to connect to the notion of selling cancer treatment. But when you've been given the possible death-sentence diagnosis of cancer, you want help. And you want to survive. And there is certainly joy in the survival.

When you have cancer, and find yourself facing a sea of big, impersonal sounding clinic names and ego-driven surgeon specialists, there's at least one choice that makes it clear that the most important person in this equation is the patient. Are you scared? Want a friend with a cure?

One to One Cancer Treatment Center is here for *you*.

It's all about you. Like the tag line says, "It's personal."

And sub-textually, it's also about One to One taking your challenge personally. What more could you ask for in a time of crisis?

One to One gets prospects past their fear of making the wrong choice with an intensely personalized focus.

Once the patient chooses One to One, their life is better by the degree that they feel cared for, they feel as if they're in good hands, and they feel hope.

The patient leaves feeling as if they matter.

In this case, the owner's joy is in not only making people better, but in making them *feel* better. He fancies himself the old-time, country doctor of high-tech cancer treatment. When a scared patient who feels like life is spinning out of control meets a cancer doctor who is willing to give out his personal cell phone number, will accept a call for any reason, and is even willing to make house calls, it can give a patient a degree of calm. Where some doctors have so much ego that it seems there's room in the relationship only for them and what they want, this doctor knows the most important person is you, the patient. We've been told that many doctors apparently treat cancer victims as if they're already dead. This doctor doesn't. They're still here, and he honors them.-

THE SPECTRUM OF BRAND-INFLUENCED DECISION MAKING

Let's admit it: more often than not, buying decisions are far from earthshaking. Nonetheless, those less life-changing, more day-tweaking decisions are often still based on fear.

Like the "fear" of the wrong hamburger experience.

That's a pretty low-grade fear.

Frazzled and afraid your kids are going to be unhappy during their meal? McDonald's makes sure it's the happy place. Mom needs to know that there's a Happy Meal with her child's name on it.

Afraid of having a lousy burger? That's why Burger King, whether it's for better or for worse, hammers on the idea of flame-broiled Whoppers. It's just going to be a better tasting burger.

Afraid of not having your little burger luxury and being able to revel in the experience? Carl's Jr. (or Hardee's, depending on your market) is there for you. They claim that "if it doesn't get all over the place, it doesn't belong in your face." It's an inconsequentially decadent experience to claim as your own or to revel in with your equally decadent, burger-loving friends.

Fear of having unhappy kids. Make my kids happy.

Fear of having a lousy burger. Make my burger taste better.

Fear of having a mundane meal. Make my meal decadent and noteworthy.

Fear of a lousy haircut. Make my haircut easy with people who care.

Fear of the wrong eye doctor. Make my eye doctor be approachable and skilled.

Fear of the wrong cancer clinic. Make my clinic treat me like I matter.

On this escalating scale of fears, we haven't once used fear as a motivator. But what we have done is recognized the fear and presented a way to undermine it. There aren't many places you'd want to undermine a prospect—but there's certainly nothing wrong with undermining a fear with a positive and useful counterbalance.

Feel their fear.

Feel your joy.

Take it to the brand—which ultimately leads to the bank.

IGNITION POINTS

- Fear prevents prospects from acting and becoming customers; part of the job of a brand is to help prospects feel comfortable and get past the fear.
- The first question to be answered is: Why does what you love doing matter to your customer?
- The next question: How will you get your prospect past their fear of acting?
- The final question: How do you want your customer to feel when he or she leaves your business?
- A brand has to, in part, make a promise to the customer that his or her life will be better.
- A weak brand can inspire doubt and inaction on the part of a prospect.
- If a weak brand makes the prospect feel nothing, he's likely to do nothing.
- There is a full spectrum of fears about purchasing decisions—from insignificant to life altering.

- Addressing a low-grade fear, such as fear of buying the wrong hamburger, is not about changing anyone's life—but it should be considered in determining the brand.
- Fear of choosing the wrong cancer doctor is a matter of life and death—and is an absolutely essential consideration in determining the brand.
- Feeling their fear and your joy, and successfully finding the intersection, will result in a resonant brand.

FIRESTARTER

Think of three brands that you find really attractive—brands that not only appear solid, but are actually attractive. A fine example of this would be eHarmony, a brand which is so strong it makes some people think, Gosh, if I were single again… What is it about these three brands that are inviting? What is it that makes them speak to you, and put aside any possible fears you might have about patronizing these businesses—or, perhaps, has made you use them?

Chapter 12

ONCE UPON A BRAND

So, customer fear, workplace joy, your brand—how do you figure all this out? It's understandable if this all seems a bit daunting. But you can do it. And in many ways, you already have more meat for your brand than you realize. In fact, you're wired to discover your brand. That wiring comes in the form of the oldest mode of communication known to man: storytelling.

WHAT'S IN A STORY?

Everything. It's the oldest form of communication for a reason. At its best, storytelling is potent and charged with meaning. *The Bible*, certainly one of the oldest and most widely distributed books in the world—and certainly one of the most influential—is a compilation of stories. Same with the *Book of Mormon*, the *Talmud*, the *Koran*, the *Bhagavad Gita*, Aesop's Fables, the Greek and Roman myths, and any of a number of other writings by which humans have run their lives. Stories matter.

You have stories of why you're in the business and how you've helped people in your business. They are an incredibly useful tool in helping to break down who you are. Many of our clients have used their own stories as integral components to building their own brands.

As it happens, some of our own clients have incredibly poignant brand stories. For instance, Susan Graham of Senior Edge Legal had tapped into her personal story and was already using it before we began her re-branding effort. This is the story as she had originally published it:

> I was like most little girls when growing up – I was in love with my father. When I grew up and moved away from home I talked with my parents every Sunday afternoon.
>
> After my husband returned from service in the Marines in Vietnam, we moved from Buffalo, New York to Idaho. He started law school. We spent the first few weeks buying a home and fixing it up. One Saturday my mother called and told me that my father was missing. The next day she called and said he had committed suicide.
>
> My world stopped!
>
> I was devastated. My mother was inconsolable in her grief. My husband and I went back east as fast as we could and tried every way to help her. She was in despair. At her request, we left school, sold our home and moved back to help with the family business. Every day I went to work my mother was on the floor crying. I tried to find help. I knew I did not have the experience or skills to know what needed to be done or how to do it. There were no professionals that I could find to help - no lawyer, no counselor, no doctor, no family. No one was able to offer support and common sense wisdom. After one month my mother fired my husband, and I lasted three months. After that, my mother and I rarely spoke before she died 8 years later.
>
> I returned to the West, so saddened that I could not find help or assistance to ease my mother's distress or help myself through this awful time.
>
> That was the beginning for me to understand the pain and confusion when someone dies. Since that time, with

> training and experience, I have developed a law practice that specializes in helping families protect their assets, independence and loved ones during the good days, and the impossibly bad days when someone dies, or becomes incapable of caring for themselves. Through these hard lessons I learned how to set up plans to protect and guide families in difficult personal times.

This story, heart-wrenching as it is, helped inform Ms. Graham's brand. Like many small business owners, she spent years successfully operating under a common kind of default brand: a law office with her name on a sign out front. She knows who she is and what she wants to accomplish.

Eventually, she'll want to sell the business.

And selling the business with her name out front, if she's not planning on continuing with the business, is a challenge.

It would be much easier to sell the business if the name of the company is something other than hers.

Through listening to her story and talking to her about what she does and why, and after many, many hours of brainstorming and deliberation and a formal exploratory process with Susan Graham, the name of the company became Senior Edge Legal. Tagline: It's your turn. The logo is a contemporary and stylized graphic of green grass, with the company name in graduated shades of green. It's optimistic and inviting.

The company is all about using legal means to give senior citizens an edge in their estate planning. These are people who've worked hard for a living, have retired, and have an estate worth roughly one- to three-million dollars. They don't want to do anything fancy. They just want to enjoy life as retirees and grandparents without worry. It's their turn to live well.

But the prospective clients are also often uneasy. They worry about their estate. They worry about what might happen. The golden years have a tarnished edge because of those nagging doubts. Stories like Susan Graham's are not uncommon. The difference is that Ms. Graham's story profoundly influenced her career path, putting her on the road to doing her best to make sure what happened to her family doesn't happen to anyone else's.

Senior Edge Legal. "It's your turn." A logo of optimistic green.

It's a brand destined to offer a happy ending to the story.

SEE THE DIFFERENCE?

We spent quite a lot of time listening to Dr. Samuel Giveen tell his story. When asked about what inspired him to become an optometrist, he related this story…

> When I was a kid, I spent a lot of time in an optometrist's office. Fifth and sixth grade, I had a vision, eye-teaming problem that was dealt with through weekly and bi-weekly vision sessions with an optometrist. So we got very close. And it helped out a lot. I had an eye that wanted to cross and he got things so that it didn't happen. He had all these exercises he'd send me home with. I'd do them every day. Spend 20 or 30 minutes a day doing these exercises. They worked.

Dr. Giveen also mentioned at one point that there are two main things patients worry about. We asked him to elaborate, and he said, "One of my instructors told me when I was in school, 'If you go from the place of figuring that when a patient walks in the office, they're afraid they're going to go blind, and they're afraid you're going to fleece them, then that's a good place to start. You need to make sure you're giving them good care, you're taking reasonable precautions financially that nothing bad is going to happen and you're being reasonable about things, and you have to make sure the patient knows that. I never forget that advice. It's good advice."

And considering that one of his offices is in a lower income area, this advice has probably served him well. The people are less well-educated and have less money. Good advice indeed.

And then, there are the cases that "you write home about."

Dr. Giveen said,

> This woman comes in. She's about 23, and she has this apparent eye turn. She came in with her mother, and her mother said, "Oh, yeah. She's had that since she was about six months old."
>
> And she's 23 now. She's had eye exams every 3 or 4 years for her whole life, and she saw very poorly with that eye. It was actually fairly disfiguring her appearance. And by the end of the exam, which probably took 20 minutes in her case, I'm sitting down with her and her mother, and I'm telling them, "She doesn't have an eye turn. Her eyes are actually straight. One of her eyes is being pushed out of the socket, and she's got a tumor behind her eye."
>
> It was a shock for her to hear this. It was a shock for her mother to hear this. She'd had five or six eye exams over 20 years. And she was told she had an eye turn. A lazy eye. And the thing was growing. And eventually it would have ruined her optic nerve and she'd have a blind eye.
>
> So, we sent her to a surgeon. They took out the tumor. They were very happy and relieved to find an answer.

Dr. Giveen described the young woman as somewhat mousy and quiet. We asked if he'd seen her again since the surgery. He said, "Two or three months ago she stopped in to say hi. She wears makeup. She's had her hair done nicely. She looked good. This kind of thing really makes me love my job."

His story is one of being inspired by a generous optometrist. It inspired him to become an eye doctor himself. One of the most important pieces of advice he ever got was from an instructor who told him the two most important things on a patient's mind are not going blind and not getting fleeced. He diagnosed a young woman with a chronic problem that had been plaguing her since birth and changed her life.

Granted, this is just the tip of the iceberg of how much we've learned about Dr. Samuel Giveen. But this is the kind of potent storytelling that led us from the sterile sounding United Eye Care Specialists to Dr. Sam's Eye Care and his "Straight talk, better vision" brand.

As with Senior Edge Legal's Susan Graham, we think the world of Dr. Sam. He's dedicated to his cause. He's on a mission. And his stories helped us get to the heart of who he is, what he stands for, and how to portray his brand.

THE DIFFERENCE IS A LOVE FOR DOING IT

The woman who owns Ooh La La Hair Studio never had any thoughts of going into hair styling as a career. In fact, she'd considered pursuing a college athletic scholarship. For various reasons, it simply didn't happen. And when her friends were all going off to college, she was sitting at home, wondering what to do next.

Interestingly, it was her aunt—who'd been a beautician—who suggested going to beauty school.

And it was something that had never crossed her mind, mainly because hair styling was something that had always been a hobby for her. She had spent her free time cutting all her girlfriends' hair. It was something she did for fun, did for her friends, did because she enjoyed doing it for people she liked.

You can really make a career out of that?

Apparently so.

And when she realized that it was possible, she threw herself at it wholeheartedly.

She was an aggressive and hungry student of hair styling. She wanted to know EVERYTHING about working with hair.

She learned so much that she was beginning to wonder what her next move was.

She asked the owner of the salon where she was working what the next step would be.

As it happens, the owner of the salon had been thinking about selling.

So, she sold the salon to her eager and enthusiastic employee.

And the eager and enthusiastic employee became an eager and enthusiastic salon owner—whose bleached blond hair and various tattoos were something of a defining brand characteristic.

It wasn't much of a stretch to take that blond, tattooed hipster persona and infuse her rebranding with a hip, tattoo-esque logo and the tagline, "Love, Truth, Hair." At its very core, this is a brand built on a woman's love for styling hair and loving the people she styles it for. And the tongue-in-cheek seriousness of the tagline speaks to her unwillingness to take any of this too seriously.

This is, after all, hair.

It's not estate planning or vision care.

It's about style.

Nonetheless, it's also an emotionally loaded proposition for a lot of people.

As mentioned earlier, there's something simultaneously amusing and disarming about the whole brand. It's a tongue-in-cheek philosophy of hair.

It puts people at ease and suggests they're in the right place.

THE DIFFERENCE IS AN OBSESSION

Just to prove that this isn't really all about life and death, that it is possible to brand a business without offering a product or service that means solving the big and dire problems in someone's life (like hair), we once worked briefly with a ski tuning service in Park City, Utah.

We actually didn't change the company name.

But we did spend a fair amount of time talking to the owner.

He was, literally, a world-class ski tuner.

Ski tuning, in case you don't know, is professionally treating the bottoms of your skis as well as the metal edges, to give you the fastest speed and most agile handling possible.

The bottoms periodically need to be ground down, they need to be waxed, and the edges need to be sharpened just so.

To some extent, ski tuning could be considered a lost art. Professional skiers and Olympic-caliber athletes certainly have access to ski tuners. But by and large, the masses who ski give their equipment to ski shops that run them through computerized, automated equipment. There isn't a lot of human involvement with the tuning process. And for the vast majority of skiers, that's probably just fine.

However, for skiers who seriously need a competitive edge, a professional human ski tuner is still the way to go.

And the company we were working with was two guys in a tiny shop with a rack full of skis and a bunch of tools. No automated equipment. These are professional ski tuners of the highest caliber.

The owner of the company was truly a ski tuner's ski tuner. He worked in many different ski shops before going to work for the US Ski Team. He spent time in Europe as a ski tuner for the women's World Cup Team.

His reputation as a ski tuner is such that he gets shipments of skis from around the globe. Someone racing in Argentina in August will pack up their skis and send them to him to be tuned for their next big race.

And, of course, being in Park City, he's surrounded by plenty of skiers, some of whom are truly world class and many others who fancy themselves as such.

When we talked to him about his business and asked him why he does what he does, he said, "I don't know how to do anything else. I don't know what else I would do if I didn't do this." He's truly a ski tuning geek of the highest order. He does one thing: makes skis as fast as is humanly possible.

We didn't have any plans to change his company name: Podium Ski Service.

If you don't know anything about sports, the podium is where you find the winners. When you place first, second or third in an event, you end up on the podium with the other two finishers.

As far as we were concerned, Podium Ski Service was the right name.

We did, however, come up with a tag line: Obsessed With Your Edge.

Obsession really is an operative concept here. We're talking about a guy who spends all day looking at the bottoms of skis. The edge is an especially critical part. If it's not tuned correctly, you don't have control.

Too sharp, and the edge is "grabby." It can pull you all over the place. Not sharp enough, and you don't have the turning ability you require. And when you're speeding through the gates and around the turns of a downhill race at 50 miles per hour, you want control and agility.

Then, of course, having your skis properly tuned gives you the edge over the competition.

The tag line is both a technical truth and an aspiration.

Interestingly, this man decided to underwrite a skiing show on the local public radio affiliate. When we wrote the underwriting mention, we used the line, "Podium Ski Service: world-class ski tuners obsessed with your edge." The public radio folks were hesitant. If you know anything about public radio underwriting, you know that you're not allowed to "sell." You can't make what are considered advertising claims. You can't say things like "we're the best." And they thought "world-class ski tuners obsessed with your edge" was somehow selling. I explained that we were talking about a man who had been a ski tuner for one of the world's most prestigious international ski racing organizations and who had toured Europe as a ski tuner to the champions. As for "obsession," it's not only hard to argue that the job is not an obsession, but the word is no more sell-y than the word used by one of NPR's biggest and most faithful underwriters, Novo Nordisk, for whom curing diabetes is a "passion."

It went on the air.

And the beauty of it is the double entendre of having better edges and gaining an edge on the competition remains intact.

Podium Ski Service might be helping to change lives—but it's doing so in a context of recreation, without the same gravity as saving a child's vision or protecting someone's life savings.

Yet the "obsessed with your edge" brand is still solid, organic, and works like a dart thrown at the core customer.

WHAT'S YOUR STORY?

Are you an obsessed hobbyist? Are you a highly schooled professional on a mission? Were you deeply influenced by a professional care provider in your youth?

You have stories about why and how you do what you do.

You have anecdotes about customers you've served and served well.

You have tales about your ideal day at work.

These are potent and important stories.

They inform your brand.

At the risk of invoking cries of sacrilege, look at *The New Testament*. Everything about this work is focused on "the brand message" of Christianity.

And before we go any further, know that this is not about preaching Christianity. Regardless of our personal beliefs, we do not proselytize about any religion other than branding. You can be Hindu, Muslim or Buddhist, and this example still holds water.

So, back to *The New Testament* and its de facto brand message.

In their book *Buck Up, Suck Up*, James Carville and Paul Begala tell a story about getting the notoriously loquacious Bill Clinton to begin speaking in sound bites. In the context of a presidential campaign, sound bites may be considered brand messages. Clinton hated sound bites. He refused to use them.

Finally, knowing his Southern Baptist heritage, Carville and Begala sat him down, handed him a Bible, and made him read John 3:16: "For God so loved the world that he gave his one and only Son, that whoever believes in him shall not perish but have eternal life." That verse is 26 words long, and it condenses the entire basis of Christianity into a single thought.

A sound bite.

That was how they got Bill Clinton, Southern Baptist, to appreciate the potency of sound bites, helping him become one of the most powerful men in the world.

Now, the point here is not so much the potency of sound bites. Rather, it's about the sound bite under discussion. That "brand" and that sound bite are informed by an entire book full of stories.

Stories are potent.

We are wired for stories.

Stories inform some of the most powerful organizations on the planet, i.e., religions.

Religions are spiritually-based organizations and they can be life-changing.

If stories can be distilled into single thoughts and are potent enough to inform life-changing spirituality, shouldn't stories be potent enough to inform your business's brand?

We're *not* telling you to start a religion. (That's another book entirely. And our good friend and persuasion guru, Dave Lakhani, who grew up in a cult, would have some choice things to say about that.)

What we *are* telling you is to dig deep and find the stories that are going to help determine your brand and make your business stronger.

IGNITION POINTS

- As a human being, you are hard-wired for stories—and story is at the core of your brand.
- Frequently, an indelible brand is built upon the business founder's personal story.
- Ideally, your brand story concerns why you do what you do, and your main difference.
- Regardless of whether you sell widgets or save lives, you have stories about why and how you do what you do.
- You have anecdotes about customers you've served and served well.
- You have tales about your ideal day at work.
- These potent and important stories inform your brand.
- Bill Clinton learned the power of the sound bite and was eventually elected to the most powerful office in the world because he was influenced by a story.

FIRESTARTER

You have a reason why you got into your business. You have experiences that capture the essence of your reason for being. You have customers whose experiences typify what you love about your work. If you could tell only one story about your business, what would it be?

Chapter 13

FROM DEFINING TO REFINING

We've looked at who you are. We've looked at who your customer is. We've examined the intersection. We've gone through the stories that illustrate who you are relative to your customer.

We have a lot of thoughts and a lot of words.

What now?

It's sugaring down time.

If you grew up in New England or Quebec, you probably have an idea of what sugaring down is. If it's a new expression for you, here's a little insight to the process.

In places rich with maple trees, springtime is a key time in the production of maple syrup. As the weather warms, the sap begins to rise in the maple trees. The maple trees are tapped and the sap is drawn off into buckets. (Clear plastic bags are more likely in contemporary collection, but we prefer the retro, antique style of the metal bucket.)

The buckets of sap are collected and emptied into a vat. The vat is heated to boil off enough of the water to concentrate the sap into syrup.

Depending on the concentration of the sap, it takes as much as 50 quarts of sap to make one quart of syrup.

That's quite a ratio.

Imagine if everything you did in your work on a daily basis required a 50-to-1 ratio of input to output. How productive would you ever be?

But when it comes to writing—which, in essence, is what we're doing here—it's not unusual to pour in a high ratio of sap to get out a very small quantity of highly concentrated syrup.

Or, in our case, a highly concentrated brand.

LOOK WHERE YOU ARE

You've defined quite a bit about you, your customer, and what matters most in that particular business equation.

Take what you've got, and pore over it all.

Immerse yourself in what you've written down.

Absorb all of it.

Then, put it aside.

Mull it over for a few minutes.

Consider you and your brand.

Then, take pen to paper (probably more effective than fingers to keyboard in this instance) and just start writing down what comes to mind.

Write long, run-on sentences.

Write in sentence fragments.

Write single words.

Don't concern yourself with format or style. Just make your brain work. Nobody is going to be looking at or judging this writing. It's just a way to begin the sugaring down of your work so far. You're distilling all your work up to now, looking for the essence of your brand.

When it's right, you'll know.

We sit and do this very process for all of our clients who require branding or re-branding. And believe us when we say: it's hard work.

It never comes easy.

We do the writing, and then we hash it out.

Then, we write some more.

It definitely helps to work with a partner when you do this—someone who understands the meaning of "partner," i.e., they don't negate anything. Rather, they try to build on it.

TAKING A LESSON FROM SECOND CITY

Probably the most famous of all improvisational comedy troupes is The Second City. There's a lot to learn from the work they've been doing since 1959 (yes, they were at it long before John Belushi and Eugene Levy—and improv comedy predates even The Second City). What you can take from them comes in the form of two very important words: "Yes, and…"

Yes-and'ing is also known as "going for the agreement."

It is the core of all improvisational comedy.

One does not judge, block or deny what comes out of the other performer's mouth. Instead one accepts, builds on and develops the premise.

Example:

Let's assume your partner says, "You know, what if our glass blowing business is the only one that offers free coffee? We could hang our hat on that."

Try to avoid coming back with "Coffee? What's that got to do with glass blowing? Nothing!"

That's like a verbal brick wall. It forces everything to come to a screeching halt.

Instead, try saying something like, "*Yes, and* if we offered blown glass sugar bowls for a super low price, it may be the entry point to folks then spending more."

Now, do we think this is a brilliant idea?

Not really.

But it keeps the momentum going and lets you then move on to the next thing.

This is as it should be in the development of your brand. If you're working with a partner, work together to develop the essence of what you've been defining up to now.

If you're working alone, don't judge what you write but let it all come out and try to build upon it.

When you negate something, you shut it down and prevent any further growth.

If you welcome it and build on it, regardless of how harebrained it may seem, you expand the range of possibilities and (one hopes) find the gold.

Obviously, we're not going for punch lines here, which is helpful. Dying might be easy, but comedy is really hard. Branding may not be easy, but it's definitely somewhere between ease of dying and the difficulty of comedy.

Also, branding is never harder than when you're doing it for yourself.

WE KNOW—WE BRANDED OURSELVES

On the face of it, Slow Burn Marketing might seem like a fairly obvious concept.

We are dedicated to the slow and thoughtful branding and marketing of small businesses. We do not recommend flash-in-the-pan marketing techniques that make big money in the short term, but harm the overall brand in the long term.

That isn't what Slow Burn Marketing does.

And on the face of it, our brand seems effortless.

It took us many months—twice as long as it would take us for one of our clients.

Marketing guru Roy H. Williams likes to say that when you're inside the bottle, you can't read the label.

In our opinion, even more challenging is being inside the bottle, trying to create the label that goes on the outside. That is a difficult perspective from which to work.

It's not impossible, mind you.

As we've proven.

Just know that you're embarking on a journey that is quite challenging. It is unlikely to come easily, but embrace it. If you go in knowing it's going to be difficult and you don't resist, it actually becomes easier.

AN EXAMPLE OF A BRAND DISTILLATION

We're going to offer an example of how we developed a brand and use it as a cautionary tale as well.

We were approached by a business called Innovative Practice Solutions. The company, headed by a husband and wife team, is a dental practice consultancy. They work with dental practices to make them more profitable.

Which, on the face of it, sounds very prosaic.

For IPS, it's not. We'll explain why in a moment. First, their problem.

They needed rebranding because, among other things, there's another company called Innovative Practice Solutions. And as it happens, this other Innovative Practice Solutions consults to (what else?) dental practices. Our IPS was tired of the confusion with the other IPS.

Our IPS was also familiar with our work.

So they came to us and said, "We need to be rebranded."

We said, "OK."

And so the process began.

We sat down with the husband and wife team, Lenora and David Milligan. We had to talk with them, find out what they're all about, where their difference lies, learn everything there is to learn about them, before beginning the long and arduous process of determining their brand.

Lenora began this company some years back when she realized that, without a dental degree, there was only so far she was ever going to be able to go in the dental business. But that wasn't before she had run a highly profitable practice of her own—which she lost when some nefarious business partner pulled the rug out from under her. So, not only is Lenora intimately familiar with the running of a dental practice, she's also intimately familiar with how one can lose a dental practice. She has Experience with a capital "E."

Her husband David comes from the oil fields of the American Southwest. After working as a roughneck, he eventually turned to inside sales for an industrial packaging company, and ultimately went to work for his wife. That's the condensed version, for sure. But let it suffice to say that, prior to IPS, there is no dental experience on his side—only real life, hands-on, git-'er-done stick-to-it've-ness. Much like his wife, David knows how to take care of himself and make things happen.

In a nutshell, those are the people at the helm of the business. They have some employees, but they're the principals.

As for the business model, that's a whole other story.

We've described their operation as a consultancy. Unfortunately, in the world of dental practices, much like elsewhere, "consultant" is a dirty word. You've probably heard some version of the joke that a consultant is someone who borrows your watch, tells you what time it is, keeps the watch, then sends you a bill for it. (If you're a consultant, please don't send us hate mail. If you haven't already figured it out, we are also consultants.) By and large, consultants in the dental practice arena are often regarded by dentists with a jaundiced eye.

That said, the Milligans are a different kind of consultancy.

Frequently, dental practice consultancy works this way: the consultant has the dentist sign a two-year contract for his services. Then, the consultant comes and spends four days onsite with a dentist. Next, he gives the dentist a list of problems to be corrected, volumes of instructional material to be digested, and goes home—but often, not before telling the dentist which staffers must be fired. Then, each week, the dentist and the consultant have a phone call to discuss the progress the dentist is making and talk about how to meet various challenges.

The Milligans do not work that way.

For starters, they have no contracts. Their clients remain clients at will. As Lenora has said, "If someone can't hand me that check with a smile each month, I don't want it."

Next, they are very much hands on. They do not spend four days on site, then conduct their business remotely. Instead, they are in a client practice every other week, working with the dentist and his team to create a smoother, better functioning unit. They rarely tell a dentist who needs to be fired. Instead, they try to work with the existing core team members in an effort to improve their performance and do a better job. Suggesting dismissal is a last resort.

They put a tremendous amount of emphasis on communication. After all, their clients are people who spent their education learning to be skilled dentists. They were never schooled in the business of running a business—management, delegation, team building, patient relations and, of course, communication skills.

The bottom line is that, at the end of the first year of business with a new client, they've typically increased the bottom line by 35%.

But there's an even bigger payoff: everyone who works in the practice, from the dentist on down to the receptionist, is living a better life. Why? Because the skills they've learned at work can't help but spill over into their personal lives. Lousy communication is at the core of so many problems that people experience on a daily basis. What these people are learning from the Milligans and their team members is how to be a better communicator and, ultimately, a better person.

There's also a commonality between Slow Burn Marketing and Innovative Practice Solutions. We've joked that in our business, we specialize in turning down new clients. The Milligans have a similar business model. They are not for everyone. They don't wear suits, they don't talk in consultant-speak, and they don't try to please all dentists because it simply doesn't work. They will often turn down dentists whom they don't believe they can help.

Which, of course, makes that dentist try that much harder to hire them.

Like us, they have learned who is going to be a good fit for their particular brand of consulting. They are going to work only with someone who's in line with the model of their core client.

This, also, is very much the *Reader's Digest* version of their story. We sat and talked with them for many hours. Then, we went away, came back, spoke again, went away again and began the tedious work of plucking new business names out of the air.

WHAT'S IN A NAME?

Quite a bit—especially for a business as different as this one. If they're that different, they need a name that reflects the difference. We weren't huge fans of Innovative Practice Solutions for the simple reason that, well, it isn't innovative. This is a case where, if you have to say it, maybe it's not so.

Anyway, here now, the raw notes from both Honey and Blaine re the name change for Innovative Practice Solutions. One note: in places, we focus on the 35% business increase in year one, and changed it to 33 at one point because, as a non-round number, we thought it sounded more believable, and we liked the symmetry of "33." And be warned: none of this is pretty. Here now, the list of possible names…

Fuel 33
Core 33
Factor 33
Squad 33
Evolution 33
Group 33
Asset 33
Juice 33
Path 33
Route 33
M2
The Milligan Group
Team Milligan
The Full Milligan
Personal Advantage
Long View
Practice Plus
Threshold
Open Hand
Winning Team
Your Winning Team

Team Win
The lineup
Starting Lineup
Roster
Management pants
Team Mix
Game Day
M and M
M Squared
Dental dominance
Better Dental
Empowered Dental
Empowerment dental
The Milligan Group
Uprise Dental
L & D
Superior dental
Proof positive
evolution Dental
Your solution dental
Gravity Dental

Making the best practices better
Good, better, best
Good, better, brilliant
Haboob Dental
A List
D.A.M. : Dental Asset Management
The Full Milligan
As good as you thought it would be
As you hoped
Everything they never taught you in dental school
Personal Advantage
Humans
M.O.M. – Milligan on Milligan
High Bar
Rise
Real Deal
Custom
Dental Plan
Dental Planners
Power to the practice
Fuel 33
Core 33
Long View
Squad 35
Contingent 35
Unit 35
Team Up 35
Gang
Coalition
The Practice Posse
Sidekick
Partner
Pilot
Ascension
Waypoint
Pull
Plum
Crowning
Snap
Gravy
Salt
Boon
Vantage
Equation
Acquire
Portal 35
Shop
Seed 35
Hyper Real
Power Practice People – P3
Unique Practice
Personal Practice Resultants
Milligans After Dark
Power To The Practice
Power Practice
Practice Power
Practice Power Up
Power Performance Systems
Performance Builders
Fuel 35
Paid With A Smile
Long View Partners
Core
Core Power

See? It's really not pretty. Pulling back the curtain often isn't. But this is the reality of how the process works. If you look at any good advertising copywriter's notes on a big campaign, things look much like this. Lots of nonsense from which you'd never expect to find a multi-million-dollar ad campaign or a place on the stage at the Clio Awards.

But this is indeed how it starts.

You see a lot of repetition in there.

A lot of things that don't make a lot of sense.

Some things that are just downright silly.

The repetition is because the two of us are often thinking along the same wavelength and may even have had a previous discussion. Or because things just get written down twice. Or we liked the way one thing works and tried tweaking it to make it work differently.

Anyway, we swap our lists around and talk some more and argue and negate things (eventually, you have to start being judgmental), and things eventually come to a head. In the case of the Milligans, we ended up with three names that we thought were killer. We loved them.

It also turned out that, after performing our due diligence, those three names would absolutely not work.

It's not because they weren't good, mind you. It was because those names were already too close to other names practicing in the field or in similar fields.

This is Part 1 of the cautionary tale mentioned earlier in the chapter: you MUST do your due diligence. The internet makes it easy. You have to make sure that any name you want to use isn't already in use by someone who can cause you grief.

So, with that in mind, we went back to our lists, put our heads together, and came up with three more names.

And due diligence showed that we weren't going to be stepping on anyone's toes. We wouldn't be knowingly creating any problem for our client.

A BRIEF INTERLUDE

At this point, it's worth noting something about the creative process.

We had one name that Honey loved and Blaine hated.

We argued about it several times.

Finally, Honey said, "I can't help it. I keep coming back to this. I can't get it out of my mind."

To which Blaine said, "Well, it's hard to argue with that kind of nagging sensibility. I don't like it, but if it won't let you go, let's keep it in the mix."

All this comes as further illustration of the cautionary tale. Part 2 of the tale is this: don't dismiss "sticky."

If you're being nagged by something in your creative process, there's a reason for it. Pay attention to the nagging sensation—but make sure you're not listening to Fred or Ethel. (Notice that Blaine, as much as he didn't like the name, understood what was going on here. He let Ethel, his creative ego, step aside because the name was sticking so tenaciously to Honey.)

So, cautionary tale Part 2 aside, let's continue to the brand...

THREE POSSIBLE BRAND DIRECTIONS

There are many different ways to present a new brand. We have one that we've decided works for us and our clients. There are no doubt as many other formats as there are practitioners. We've boiled it down to an exploration of the general thinking behind the brand, followed by the presentation of three possible directions. So, here's where we went with the Milligans...

INNOVATIVE PRACTICE SOLUTIONS — SITUATION & FOCUS

THE SITUATION: Innovative Practice Solutions does not own the URL for their business name. That URL is owned by a competitor of the same name. For the simple reasons of clarity and differentiation, the name must change. Additionally, the name Innovative Practice Solutions doesn't fully represent the unique work being done here. A brand needs to be developed around a new name that lets prospects know this isn't just another rubber-stamp consulting group. What's happening here is a business changer and, often, a life changer.

PRIMARY BUSINESS FOCUS: Fulfilling the dental ideal. Showing dentists how to have the practice they imagined they'd have all those years ago when they first started on their professional journey. What we do shows a really good dentist how to have a truly successful business. In the process, the communication techniques we teach are often applied to the dentist's life. Because of this, we improve the lives of all those who interact with them.

The target demo is somewhat disillusioned. They don't know why their business isn't working the way they thought it would. The good news is: we do. We've been there, done that and seen it all. From generally poor intra-office communications, to bad or no management skills; from looking at their staff as a problem that needs to be solved, to being brow-beaten by a problem employee, We Get It. We also know how to fix it. Like many business owners, dentists spent years learning their trade without learning the *business* of their trade.

They are further frustrated by the prevailing concern (often founded) that consultants aren't to be trusted. More good news: we're not what they expect. We're here to re-define consulting. We are the one, proven, hands-on, custom solution. Custom. Hands-on. Proven. These are the three pillars of the difference we bring to the dental party.

Nothing we do is cookie cutter. Part of our long record of success stems from viewing each business as unique and singular. We craft an education and profitability plan specifically for their unique situation. We also don't treat them with an outstretched arm. Unlike most consultants, we're willing to roll up our sleeves, get in there and get dirty. Because of this approach, our results speak for themselves: an average 35% growth over the first year. Go ahead, argue with that.

INNOVATIVE PRACTICE SOLUTIONS—MISSION & GOAL

MISSION: Our mission is to make a good dental practice into a great dental practice. Because of the skills we teach them, dentists who are incredibly talented in the hands-on portion of their job also become highly engaging for patients as well as staff. We want the dentist who works with us to feel that he or she can now have the business they'd dreamed about back in dental school—a practice where patients actually look forward to a visit.

Our client dentists are then allowed to use the communication skills and inter-personal building blocks they get from us in every aspect of their lives...no extra charge.

GOAL: To make it clear that if you want your practice to be financially and personally successful, there is a list of, oh...one firm you should talk to. And, if you're already at the top of the ladder and want to stay there, there is a list of, oh...that same one firm.

Internally, the goal is to build the business model that re-defines consulting as dentists know it and then expand into other fields, both medical and non-medical.

INNOVATIVE PRACTICE SOLUTIONS — TARGET AUDIENCE

CORE TARGET: "Skilled & Compassionate Dr. Dental." A highly skilled professional who went into dentistry expecting one thing and, for some reason, is getting another. "Skilled & Compassionate Dr. Dental" is the one who learned all the important skills in dental school except one: how to run a dental business. Dr. Dental likes people and wants to make a difference, but how? The doctor must be willing to not back seat drive our efforts or this won't work, and we are prepared to tell the doctor as much.

PROBLEM: "Consultant" has become a dirty word for dentists. There are too many consulting firms charging big money for small-minded, cookie cutter solutions that simply don't work. These consultants typically show up once, get dentists to sign long-term contracts, and conduct the rest of their business from a distance, offering solutions without being close enough to truly understand the problem. Because of this, many dentists see all consultants as just another group of people out for their money. Innovative Practice Solutions needs to make it clear from the opening bell that there is something very different happening here.

The other problem a dentist often has is himself. The dentist may see problems with the staff, but not within himself. The dentist knows what he or she does, and how could anyone else tell the dentist better? Relinquishing control is not part of their make-up. Our solution has to be deferential, but firm.

TONE: Aspirational. Informed, yet accessible. Confident without chest pounding. Let dentists know they are speaking with the best, but there's no jacket required. This is "roll up your sleeves and prepare to be happy" time. Oh, and we also expect you to do the work, Dr. Dental. If you don't, we will call you on it.

BRAND DIRECTION 1

NAME: "A" Game

TAG LINE: Your Practice. Your Win.

POSITION: "A" Game is turning dental consultancy on its ear. We don't dress like other dental consultants. We don't sound like other dental consultants. We don't take the money and run like other dental consultants. What we do is bring individualized strategies for proven results. This isn't a consultancy. It's a resultancy.

WHAT IT'S ABOUT: "A" Game is in it to win it. When a dental office works with "A" Game, they can count on us to always bring just that, our A game. Because of this, we require our clients to be willing to roll up their sleeves and do the hard work. We take practices that have been performing at or below their potential and teach them the skills to make every season a winning season. What's a win? A happy staff that works together, happy patients who refer friends and family, an increase in profits, and an increase in the dentist's overall enjoyment—at work as well as at home.

"A" Game works with each dental practice as a team. Yes, the dentist is the captain (who must be willing to be coached), but if the entire team doesn't work as a unit, it doesn't function. Every member of the team must be working from the same play book, communicating well, and be willing to help the other team members. Any win is a team win.

"A" Game's confidence comes from a record of success enviable in any arena: a 35% average increase in a practice's bottom line the first year and continued increases in the years to come. We know that if a skilled dentist allows us to coach them and their team, what we deliver is a game changer. Even seemingly healthy businesses improve. Their business skills will finally match their dental skills, and the practice they had always hoped for will be within reach.

This is not what you get from the average dental consultancy. It is, however, what your practice gets from "A" Game. Your Practice. Your Win.

BRANDING DIRECTION 2

NAME: Route 35

TAG LINE: Power to the Practice

POSITION: Route 35 is a dental practice's unique road to success. The first year often finds new clients with a 35% increase in revenues. That 35% comes as a result of vastly improved communication, increased productivity, patient base growth, and better office morale and demeanor. The path to achieving these elements is the Route to success.

WHAT IT'S ALL ABOUT: Here's the bottom line: this is about more than merely the bottom line. It's about a holistic approach to better overall living. Ask any dentist and they'll say the ultimate goal is increased profits. And even an already healthy practice can be more productive. But the only road there is better people management skills. A happy, productive, motivated team means happier, more enthusiastic patients. This is at the core of profitability.

The route we provide is custom mapped for each practice, but the core philosophy is always the same. Through the years, we've learned how to identify challenges and blend the right combination of teaching & tactics. Every dental practice must learn how to communicate, appreciate and honor their patients and make them feel cared for. But not every practice receives this information in the same way. Each practice is different and we are flexible. Our only requirement is that our clients use our map. A dentist knows how to fill a tooth. We know how to run a happy, healthy and, yes, profitable practice.

Also know that we don't hand over a generic to-do list and walk away. We show up regularly. We work directly with the dentist and their staff. We see firsthand how each team best responds to our direction and adjust accordingly. We then continue to hone and reinforce. The journey is ongoing. Continued success is mapped just as carefully as the first steps.

The other big difference here? We require no long-term contracts. If a practice is a place where people enjoy their work, if the patients are happy to refer their friends, and the balance sheet reflects it, our clients remain clients at will. The ultimate route to profitability is the people at the practice's core. Power to the Practice.

BRAND DIRECTION 3
NAME: Salt
TAG LINE: Savor Success.

POSITION: Salt Dental Practice Management works with dental practices that already have good technical dental skills, and brings the flavor: great practice management and communication skills. This pairing of profit building and team building with solid dental technique results in the practice they always hoped for. Very tasty.

WHAT IT'S ALL ABOUT: Salt DPM is about everything they never teach in dental school. Cleaning, caps and fillings are all necessary skills. But so are communication, strategy, making a staff feel vital, and making the patient feel cared for. This is the seasoning that turns a good dentist into the heart of a thriving dental practice.

Salt DPM has achieved great results for clients by doing what most of our competitors don't: we show up regularly and individualize our teaching. It's hands-on, and we continue to taste test as we go. You don't want to over- or under-season. Also, if a practice is already doing well, we work with them to make minor but meaningful and lasting improvements that take them to an even tastier place.

And believe us when we say: we are worth our salt. Our dental industry track record averages a 35% increase in the client's bottom line the first year. Then we work with businesses to maintain or even build on that success in the years to come. Also, we don't require that dentists sign a 2-year contract. When you produce results, you don't need contracts. But if we're going to be worth our salt, we require that you are worth yours. This works only if you work.

Lastly, if you question the importance of salt, consider its import. Salt is essential for life. For thousands of years, Salt has represented qualities like Vitality, Loyalty, Friendship, Truth and Wisdom. And, in the Salt Satyagraha, Gandhi defied the British Empire so the Indian people would be free to make and use their own salt. Salt matters so much, it was historically controlled by kings and the ruling elite. Taking something good and making it better is always worthwhile—and that is the job of salt. Happier staff, more loyal patients, a fuller life. From good to better to brilliant. Salt DPM is about giving you the ability to truly savor your success.

WHAT HAPPENS NEXT...

After a presentation, we always encourage the client to sleep on it and see how they feel about things by the light of a new day. And this is important, because things will percolate in there overnight, and good things will rise to the top.

The "safe" choice here, if you haven't already figured it out, was "A" Game. It's not a particularly surprising metaphor, but solid and accurate. More importantly, it's unique. Nobody in the dental practice management consulting field appears to be using it.

The one that divided Blaine and Honey was Route 35. Blaine thought the imagery was too literal, and too inextricable from the fabled Route 66. Honey kept offering counter arguments—but what finally tipped the scale was her claim that it wouldn't leave her alone. So it was in the presentation. And based on the clients' reaction, it was a good thing.

This also serves as Part 3 of the cautionary tale: you will NEVER please everyone all the time. Don't try.

The risky choice here, if you haven't already deduced as much, was Salt. This is a completely out-of-left-field, totally unexpected, dangerous option—dangerous because it could make certain people (i.e., the client) uncomfortable.

Interestingly, it didn't seem to make the Milligans uncomfortable at all. They did exactly what we expected: looked at it, scratched their heads for a few moments, then eventually began to smile.

After it was all presented, we sent the Milligans away and told them to sleep on it.

While their reaction to Route 35 was quite positive, we'd anticipated that they'd probably go with "A" Game, the safer choice. We were surprised when they came back and said that they wanted to become Salt.

At this writing, Innovative Practice Solutions is in the process of becoming Salt Dental Practice Management. They're excited and doing little dances in secret. One of the things that really attracted them to Salt was the historical importance of salt itself. For instance: did you know the word "salary" has its roots in salt? It is believed by some historians that its etymology stems from a tradition of paying Roman soldiers in salt—which, at the time, was a precious commodity and difficult to come by. Also, for a business that serves many Indian clients, the Gandhi reference didn't hurt.

And know that this was not the end for the Milligan branding process. Next came a logo exploratory followed by the creation of a brand manifesto. The manifesto further hones in on all elements of their brand and includes a styåle guide on which all visual communications would be based. But for the purposes of this exercise, the foundation of the brand is where the meat is.

WHY ARE WE TELLING YOU ALL THIS?

While we're not showing you EVERYTHING that goes into developing a brand (that would fall somewhere on the scale of desirability right between making laws and making sausage), we want to give you some idea of how coming up with a brand (usually) doesn't just happen with the snap of a finger.

Even in those very rare instances when it does happen with a snap, chances are it's the byproduct of days if not months of mulling over the challenge.

We want to underscore that, like anything else that's worthwhile, it doesn't come easily. You will likely fail a hundred times before you finally hit the nail on the head.

We also want to point out that there is often no one solution to the problem. We've just shown you three possible approaches to a single challenge.

All three very different.

Any of the three could have easily been further developed and done the job.

And, finally, a recap of the cautionary tale.

Part 1: do not be too judgmental in the early efforts. Being too judgmental about a gestating brand is like saying the baby is ugly based on the sonogram. It's impossible to know anything at such an early stage.

Part 2: always pay attention to anything that is so sticky it won't let go of your psyche. After all, the one thing you want a brand to do is stick to the customer's psyche. If it's sticking in your brain and won't let go, there's a chance it'll do the same for your prospects.

Part 3: never expect to please 100% of people with your brand direction. In this case, we had two experienced professionals in total disagreement over a brand name. It was only an understanding of Part 2, stickiness, that helped resolve the debate.

INSTANCES WHERE THINGS DIDN'T GO SO SMOOTHLY

Both Blaine and Honey have worked in various professional capacities in which they've witnessed clients flailing about when it comes to the creative work.

In fact, one of the key phrases to watch out for is, "I'm open to anything."

Nine times out of 10, it means they're open to nothing, and either fear or ego (or both) will come barreling down upon the proceedings to quash anything that's too good.

Also, as business partners, Blaine and Honey together have done at least one brand presentation that went smashingly. We've touched on this previously. The client laughed. The client enjoyed the directions. The client went off to think about it.

And the client promptly went berserk.

What had been received so well, and should have been a simple matter of deciding which direction was best, became something else: an ever-growing list of problems and reasons why the proposed brands were entirely unsuitable.

What began as delight turned into fear and loathing...and ego.

Perfectly suitable directions were being turned away as completely unusable.

Moreover, in their place, the client kept suggesting wildly inappropriate options—things that were either lame, uninspired, middle-of-the-road nonsense, or harsh, judgmental, accusatory screed, all in the name of brand.

The client was mortified at the prospect of doing what needed to be done.

All this to say…

COMMITTING TO A BRAND IS SCARY

It is entirely possible that you will hit on the perfect brand concept.

You will then be mortified by it.

It happens.

Why?

It could be any number of reasons.

Fear of commitment.

Fear of being wrong.

Fear of not being perfect.

Fear of flying.

Fear of music.

OK, well, not the last two. Those are titles of an Erica Jong novel and a Talking Heads album, respectively.

But fear definitely plays a significant part here.

And if you go back to Chapter 8, you'll recall our warnings about Fear & Ego. We renamed them Fred & Ethel to underscore their pointlessness in this context.

And in this case quite specifically, fear is the enemy.

Just like stepping out and starting your business, this effort requires courage.

If you've read this far, you have the courage. The weak-willed left us long ago, and are busy sitting alone somewhere, muttering to themselves about how they're special and we just don't understand them.

In one way or another, the two of us combined have been doing this work for almost half a century. We've seen it all before. It's also one of the things that made us realize that every business, regardless of its size, has one commonality: people.

People are there making the decisions.

That includes the decisions about the marketing.

So that marketing is at the mercy of the people who command the ship.

As a result, those companies get the marketing they deserve.

Sometimes, that ship gets driven onto a reef and breaks apart.

Not yours, though.

Because you've come this far. You've worked with us. You're getting the picture. And you know it won't come easily, but you're ready to work at it with courage.

You will put your heart into it.

You will hone in on that one way you want people to feel about your business.

And you will get the brand that you deserve.

So go forth.

Build a brand.

Conquer the world.

IGNITION POINTS

- The sugaring down process involves boiling maple sap into maple syrup at a 50:1 ratio.
- Taking what you know about your business and distilling it into a brand is an intellectual sugaring down process.
- In "sugaring down" your brand, don't be judgmental, merely let the information flow and edit it later.
- There's an important lesson in improv comedy: learn the skill of "yes and…" going for the agreement.
- Going for the agreement without judgment helps build ideas.
- Negating something shuts it down and prevents any further growth.

- Encouraging even harebrained ideas can often yield gold.
- Be prepared: branding yourself is a challenging task.
- It's possible to write down hundreds of potential names and thousands of words before hitting on The One Brand.
- Getting to The One Brand is not pretty, but is entirely necessary—which is why you need to go for the agreement without judging anything too early.
- Once you believe you've hit on The One Brand, due diligence is necessary—it might seem like genius, but you also might not be the first genius to do it.
- You are not required to do a formal brand presentation—but you are required to know all of the elements of your brand: whom you're talking to, how you're talking to them, what your tag line is, and what you want your customer to feel about your brand.
- No matter how harebrained it may seem, always pay attention to something so sticky it won't let go of your psyche.
- This process requires courage.

FIRESTARTER

Take a pen and paper, and begin writing down stories about you and your business. Stories about how you got into it and, more importantly, why you got into it. Stories about your customers. Stories about a good day at work. Don't judge. Just write. See if a pattern or a common theme emerges. If you had to pick only one story to represent how and why you do business, which one would it be? How can you distill that story down to its essence, down to a simple statement about your reason for being in your line of work?

AFTERWORD

We've repeated this throughout the book, and we're going to say it yet again: this process called branding is hard work and it requires courage.

By venturing into this book, and especially by coming this far, you have proven yourself unafraid of hard work.

You've also proven a willingness to muster the courage it takes to commit and to beat back Fred & Ethel.

We applaud you.

As stated way back at the beginning, branding is a concept about which there is intense disagreement amongst the marketing masses.

You now have ammunition to join the fight.

Resist the call to battle on the field of branding debate.

Arguing about brand is a lot of work and you don't need that kind of frustration.

Instead, put that energy to work in branding your business.

You're going to find that while it, too, is hard work, it's going to be a rewarding and valuable effort. Your business will appreciate it. So will your customers. Branding your business well leads to certainty about what you do, why you do it, and what it is your business stands for.

That certainty is a glorious thing—and it's very attractive.

Sexy, even.

For customers and for you.

Never thought about your business as sexy, did you?

So when someone tries to engage you in an argument about what branding is, you don't need to go there.

All you need to do is nod and smile, and perhaps hand them your brand's new business card.

Go forth and brand like a billion dollars.

FREE STUFF

Really? You want more? Think you can handle it? If so, if the idea of enduring regular rants about the state of the art in advertising and marketing doesn't make you break into a cold sweat, you might be ready for *Hot Points*, Blaine & Honey Parker's free weekly newsletter. Free subscriptions are available for a limited time at their website. To sign up, visit www.SlowBurnBranding.com. Or don't. Your choice.

CPSIA information can be obtained at www.ICGtesting.com
Printed in the USA
BVOW081045200912

300972BV00002B/15/P